52 WEEKS OF Uplifting Prayers and Guided Reflection FOR WOMEN

Daily Devotion and Scripture Reading to Deepen Your Relationship with God

Edmane Castor

Published by Color My Culture

Visit www.edmaneprayerwarrior.com for a freebie.

Follow me on Facebook and Instagram at Edmane Prayer Warrior

to learn more about my ministry.

This Book
Belongs to:

Acknowledgments

First and foremost, I want to acknowledge the guidance of the Holy Spirit for bringing to my heart the thought of writing this prayer book and journal for women.

To my two daughters, Tanisha and Edonine, you are a source of encouragement. You've motivated me to write these 52 weeks' worth of prayer and journal prompts. You've never ceased to motivate me to pursue my passion. I love you, ladies. To my handsome husband, Onal, thank you for always being behind the scenes and encouraging me with your amazing words of inspiration.And to my son, Max, thank you for planting ideas and pushing me to do more. I send my deepest gratitude to all of you guys.

TABLE OF CONTENTS

Introduction

"And pray in the Spirit on all occasions with all kinds of prayers and requests. With this in mind, be alert and always keep on praying for all the Lord's people." (Ephesians 6:18).

Thank you for selecting this book. I'm grateful for the chance to share in your faith in the Lord Jesus Christ, the Lord, and Savior of the Universe.

It's my hope and prayer that the contents of this book will aid and inspire you, as all of these weekly prayers are heartfelt and intended to connect you with God, who's interceding for real people with real problems. I hope and pray that the time you devote to reading and reflecting on God's word will help you grow in your faith, deepen your relationship with God, and allow you to have more meaningful prayer conversations with God.

My husband and I have been ordained and commissioned as gospel ministers for more than four decades. In 1980, when we launched our ministry, we realized that there was a great need for prayer warriors to engage in this spiritual conflict. As a result, we began our journey as prayer warriors.

In some of the locations where we worked, the need for prayer was immense. I recalled once being in a church for youth ministry with thousands of young people present. Some of them were spiritually blind due to their unknowing participation in the devil's plot. I shed tears as I listened to some of their stories and testimonies. At this meeting, I heard stories about different forms of abuse, issues with parents, rivalries with siblings and peers, family dysfunction, child neglect, envy, jealousy, and different forms of addiction such as drugs, alcohol, and gambling.

Some described their mental health problems, such as recurring nightmares, anxiety, and depression. The devil made a mess of some of these young people's lives and wanted to continue doing so. After hearing their stories and testimonies, we spent more time praying and being filled with the Holy Spirit's power in preparation for God's intervention.

We know that prayer is the only unique weapon capable of destroying Satan's kingdom and the carefully planned strategies that he employs against us.

God used us in our ministry, miracles happened, people with broken hearts were healed, marriages were fixed, infertility was turned into fertility, babies were brought to Jesus, children were reconciled with their parents, and demons were cast away.

God has led us to plead on behalf of the people we met. God is always good and faithful to His promises. This book contains prayers, and Bible verses, and encourages time for expression and reflection. Therefore, I encourage you to embark on this journey as a prayer warrior for yourself, your family, and your friends. God keeps His promises and He is dependable.

I pray that God showers His infinite blessings on you.

About this Book

This powerful prayer book of devotion and reflection can be utilized to explore God's influence on various facets of your life. Sometimes, the theme of the weekly prayer may not be directly relevant to you or your life at the moment, but parts of it can be personalized. For example, "A PRAYER TO COPE WITH DIVORCE" can be a prayer for separation or the end of a relationship.

Even though a certain subject of prayer does not pertain to you, we are obligated as Christians to pray not only for ourselves but also for others. We are called to be prayer warriors. Some people believe prayer warriors are specially called or skilled individuals. We are all called to be prayer warriors. You can engage in prayer warfare.

Prayer warriors are devoted to God, prayer, people, and the church of Christ. Therefore, we pray constantly and have faith that God will answer each prayer in accordance with His perfect will and timing.

If you are a person who wants to build a better relationship with God through prayer and reading His Words, and if you are a person who sees the value of prayer for oneself committed to praying for others, then you are a prayer warrior.

This Book is divided into Three sections:

Weekly Prayer

Each week features a prayer that I composed. It is a prayer from the heart, and I prayed for myself or a person with real problems from my past. All of the prayers are my answered prayers, and I pray that they will be your answered prayers as well.

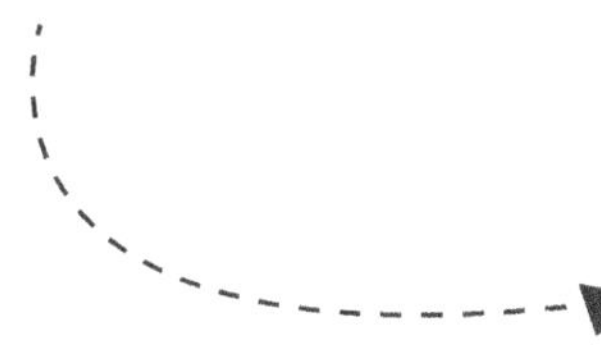

WEEK NINE: TODAY IS THE DAY OF DECISION

Eternal Father,

As I approach your throne of grace, I thank you for creating this new day.

Please help me not to be distracted, diluted, frustrated, or disappointed today. Help me to always look forward to a bright tomorrow, believing that you will take care of everything on this day that you have made and that all things will work for my good.

Today, Lord, you set before me life and death. Help me to always choose life, oh God.

Lord, guide me today in making wise decisions, carefully selecting the people in my life, and rejecting any negative thoughts that enter my mind.

Oh Holy God, help me to recognize that I am beautiful, intelligent, and wanted. Your grace is sufficient for me, God. I cannot make it on my own but I can do everything because you are my strength.

Please, let me know that I am your choice. Yahweh, guide me today to find my heart's desire and solutions to my problems. Today, my father assist me in refusing any kind of abuse from those who only want to harm me. Today, guarantee me your strength, your healing, and your comfort. Today, baptize me again with the Holy Spirit.

Lord, anoint me. Lord, I come asking that you heal those around me with broken hearts, relieve those that feel oppressed, and ease the suffering of the outcasts.

Today, Lord, help me to be optimistic and listen to your voice.

Please help me to recognize the thoughts that are not helpful to me. Allow only Your words to enter my mind and thoughts.

In Jesus Christ's most precious name.

Amen.

Weekly Reflection

Do you appreciate and cherish the life God has given you?

Do you know who God created you to be and rejoice in that?

I hope you know that you are loved. Are you having difficulty loving yourself?

Are you having negative thoughts, or feeling like you don't have much worth?

We are all sinners who have done some things we are not proud of. God does not want us to spend our lives thinking negatively about ourselves or feeling worthless.

God loves you and has a high value on your life. He wants you to remember that you are the most important thing to Him. He wants you to dedicate your life fully to Him.

Well, today is the day.

God wants you to embrace this day and make a decision to serve Him.

You can choose to serve God

Have you dedicated your life to serving God?

What are some ways you can serve God at home, work, or in your community?

Weekly Reflection

Each week contains an area for weekly reflection with questions inspired by the weekly prayer. These questions are there to help you dig deep and connect with God.

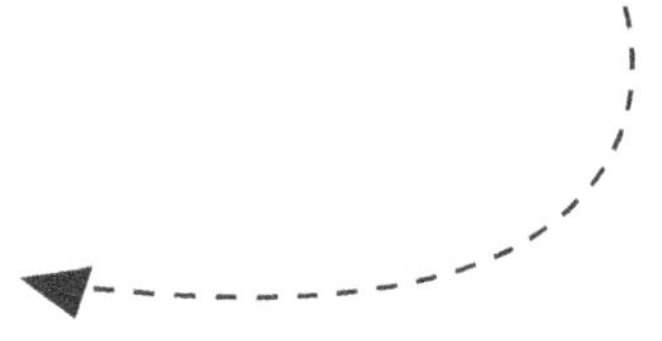

Daily Scripture/Reflection and Devotion

A daily Bible scripture is provided for reading and reflection. Occasionally, daily prompts may promote devotion and reflection. As you read and contemplate His words, ask God how you may apply them to your life. Request that He gaze into your heart and reveal any areas of Himself that require light.

You can choose to record your notes, prayer, or reflection. You can also use daily devotion as an opportunity to express what's on your mind as you read the Bible verse of the day and share your thoughts as God reveals new truths. You can complete it daily or weekly.

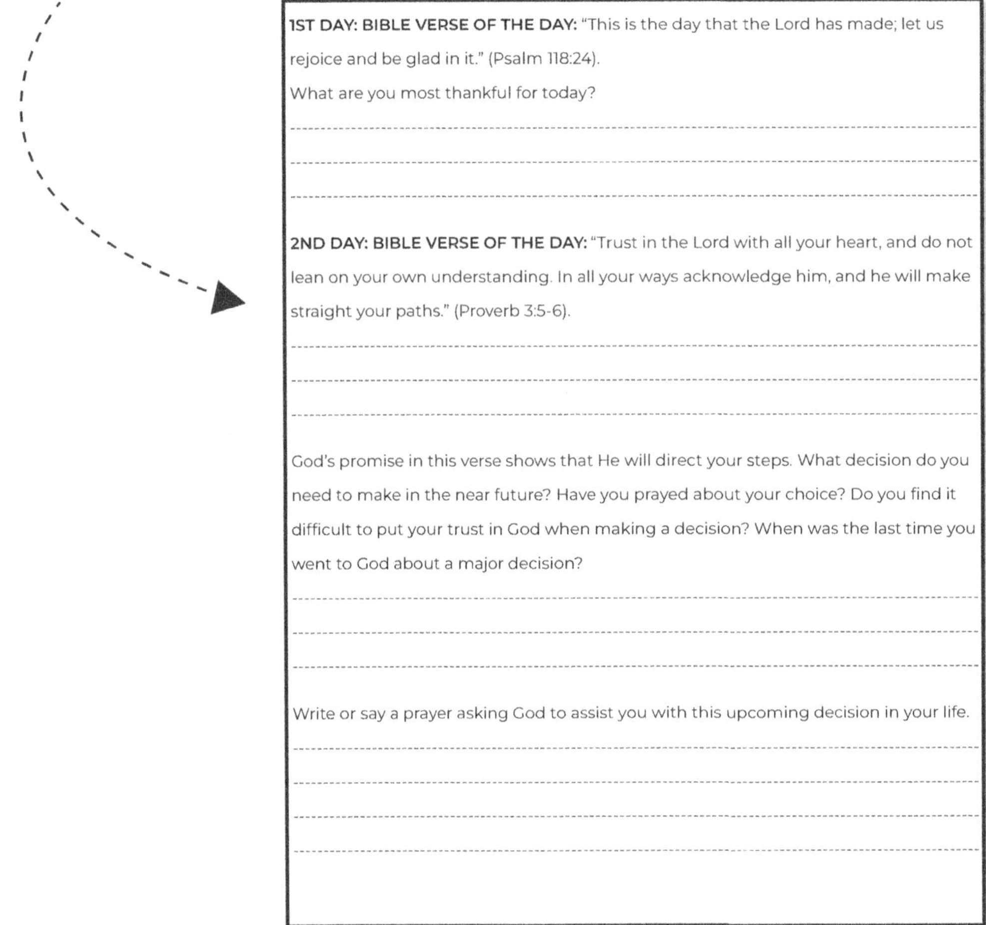

1ST DAY: BIBLE VERSE OF THE DAY: "This is the day that the Lord has made; let us rejoice and be glad in it." (Psalm 118:24).

What are you most thankful for today?

2ND DAY: BIBLE VERSE OF THE DAY: "Trust in the Lord with all your heart, and do not lean on your own understanding. In all your ways acknowledge him, and he will make straight your paths." (Proverb 3:5-6).

God's promise in this verse shows that He will direct your steps. What decision do you need to make in the near future? Have you prayed about your choice? Do you find it difficult to put your trust in God when making a decision? When was the last time you went to God about a major decision?

Write or say a prayer asking God to assist you with this upcoming decision in your life.

During these 52 weeks, you will have an opportunity to observe your growth and transformation into a spiritual prayer warrior as God moves with you and answers your prayers. Also, you would have to deepen your relationship with God through reading scripture daily, and weekly reflection.

This book can be tailored to your specific requirements based on your relationship with God. Even though this book is divided into 52-week installments for a year, I encourage you to work at your own pace. When possible, do set aside time each week or each day.

What is Prayer?

Prayer is simply an open conversation with God in which you trust that He will guide you in whatever you do and wherever you go. It is about establishing an intimate relationship with God. It is a way to open your heart to receive God's presence while He ministers to you. Prayer is a simple expression of gratitude addressed to the Maker of the universe.

It merely opens your heart and invites Him to take full control of you. Prayer is having faith in Him no matter the circumstances. I will trust in God. Even though He knows you inside and out, and your name is engraved on the palm of His hands, God still wants to hear from you. Daily prayer requires work on the part of some of us, and it can feel like a burdensome obligation at times. Prayer can be thought of as food for your body. Prayer can help you get closer to God and make your relationship with Him stronger.

Prayer does not need to be elaborate or fancy. It is a dialogue with the God of the universe.

In the Bible, there are countless people inspired to pray for a myriad of burning issues. Their prayers have been answered. God is still in the business of answering earnest prayers. James reminds us in (James 4:2) that "you don't have it, because you don't ask," and John says in (John 16:24) that "until now, you have not asked for anything in my name. Ask and you will receive, and your joy will be complete."

WEEK ONE: CELEBRATING GOD 'S GOODNESS

Dear Heavenly Father,

Be magnified! Be glorified because you are Lord of the earth. You are Yahweh. You are the King of kings and Lord of lords. Glory and honor belong to you O Lord!

At the beginning of this New Year, I stand before you to confess my sins and bring my need to your presence. Please, Father, your guidance is needed as I face the future. I don't know about tomorrow, but one thing I am certain of is that I am in your secure hands.

Thank you for your promise of goodness and mercy throughout this New Year and the coming year.

Thank you also for the assurance that I need not be afraid, for You are with me.

Help me rejoice in the day, month, and year that you have created, knowing that "your rod and your staff will comfort me." (Psalms 23:4). I will not be afraid, even in the depths of darkness.

In this New Year Lord, I claim all the plans you have in store for me and for my family to be accomplished in the wonderful name of Jesus.

At the beginning of this New Year, I proclaim life over my family, my friends, my church, my community, my country, and all those in need. I pray in the powerful name of Jesus.
Amen.

Weekly Reflection

Happy New Year!

I wish you and your family a year filled with happiness, love, good health, joy, and prosperity. This New Year should be filled with enormous surprises, and bouts of laughter. I hope that you are able to accomplish all your goals and realize your deepest desires.

This New Year, I hope the following for you:

May you embrace the divine word of God.

May you seek God's kingdom first in everything that you do.

May God's goodness and mercy accompany you throughout this year.

May you be spared from all difficulties.

Remember that God will fulfill His promises even in difficult situations and when it seems impossible.

The Bible states in (Psalms 65:11) that "You crown the year with your bounty; your wagon tracks overflow with abundance." Abundant Blessings to you and your loved ones.

Let us give thanks for this New Year with a grateful heart. What are you thankful for this New Year? List all of the things that you are thankful for this New Year.

Bring all of your worries to God for this New Year. Cast them all to Him. Take a moment to reveal those worries.

What is your offering to God for the New Year?

What's your request of God this year? Bring your requests before the Lord.

Tell everything to Jesus. Write or say your New Year prayer.

1ST DAY: BIBLE VERSE OF THE DAY: "But seek first the kingdom of God and his righteousness, and all these things will be added to you." (Matthew 6:33).

We seek God first when we seek comfort, strength, and reassurance from Him.

We put God first when we worship, praise, thank, and depend on Him rather than ourselves or others.

God has a wonderful plan for you this year. You can get a fresh start this New Year.

This year, what can you do to seek God's Kingdom and His righteousness?

2ND DAY: BIBLE VERSE OF THE DAY: "Remember not the former things, nor consider the things of old. Behold, I am doing a new thing; now it springs forth, do you not perceive it? I will make a way in the wilderness and rivers in the desert."
(Isaiah 43: 18-19).

Dwelling on the past entails relieving the same story over and over again, yet hoping for a different outcome. It reopens old wounds and prevents progress. Life will move forward whether you are ready or not. For many dwelling on their past is the biggest impediment to moving forward. The Lord is against you dwelling on your past because doing so can get you to get stuck and miss out on His blessings and all the wonderful things He has planned for you.

Are you still dwelling on your past? It might be a past mistake, a negative memory, what you consider to be a failure, a former relationship, or a decision you now regret. What are you doing to address and get over your past? Have you spoken to your church leader about it, a Christian counselor, or a life coach? Most importantly, have you brought it to God?

Your past is not who you are now. Bring everything to God and hand it over to Him. Let your past go and embrace your future in Christ.

If you are still struggling with your past, write or say a prayer asking God to help you move on from the past.

If you have moved on and no longer dwell on your past, write or say a prayer of thanksgiving. Take the time to thank God for helping you to move on from your past.

3RD DAY: BIBLE VERSE OF THE DAY: "Blessed be the God and Father of our Lord Jesus Christ! According to his great mercy, He has caused us to be born again to a living hope through the resurrection of Jesus Christ from the dead." (1 Peter 1:3).

Let God's word speak to you today! What is your definition of living hope?

Be present and take the time to write or say a short prayer thanking God for living hope.

4TH DAY: BIBLE VERSE OF THE DAY: "But you are a chosen race, a royal priesthood, a holy nation, a people for his own possession, that you may proclaim the excellencies of him who called you out of darkness into his marvelous lights." (1 Peter 2:9).

Let God's word speak to you now. Silence everything around you. Be still and meditate. What did the Holy Spirit reveal to you?

5TH DAY: BIBLE VERSE OF THE DAY: "Oh give thanks to the LORD; call upon his name; make known his deeds among the peoples!" (Psalm 105:1).

Reflect and praise God for His goodness and mercy. Take the time to think about all of His blessings on you. Write or say a prayer of thanks and praise.

6TH DAY. BIBLE VERSE OF THE DAY: "But from there you will seek the Lord your God and you will find him, if you search after him with all your heart and with all your soul." (Deuteronomy 4:29).

How can you pursue the Lord, your God, with greater zeal?

What can you do today to help you feel God's presence in your life?

Take the time to pray and ask God to make you more intentional in your pursuit of Him today.

7th Day: Bible Verse of the Day: Select one of your favorite Bible verses and meditate on the words. Spend some time in the Bible seeking one if you don't already have one.

This week, was there anything you read, prayed about, or experienced that surprised you?

BENEDICTION: "May He grant you your heart's desire and fulfill all your plans!" (Psalm 20:4).

WEEK TWO: HOW TO BE PROSPEROUS

Most Precious Lord,

I bow down before you to worship and adore you because you are the Alpha and the Omega, the Beginning, and the End. You are Yahweh, You are Mighty, and You are excellent. You always make provisions for me.

Even though life is unpredictable and uncertain, you show me the way to be prosperous, by just keeping "the book of the law on my lips and doing everything written in it. (Joshua 1:8).

Please, Father, help me not to neglect this one most needful thing in my life because I aspire to be successful in my work and personal endeavors as well as be a virtuous woman for my family and my community in whatever I do. In reference to (Deuteronomy 28:13), I desire to be the head, not the tail. I want to be above, not beneath.

That is your promise, and I take you at your word. Today, I claim it in the mighty Name of Jesus.

While I remain obedient to this command, I declare that I will succeed and experience your favor in your name. I declare that I will become everything you created me to be in the name of Jesus. I surely declare favor and grace will follow me every moment of my life. I thank you for forgiving my sins and answering my prayer. I pray in the marvelous name of Jesus.

Amen.

Weekly Reflection

God wants you to prosper. Many believe "prosperity" only means "money".

Prosperity includes physical, emotional, and spiritual well-being. Prosperity comes from God's favor and blessings. How can you be prosperous as a Christian? We can be prosperous when we put God first. If we seek God and do good work, He will bless us. Working hard and putting forth effort is essential because desire alone will not allow you to prosper.

In what areas of your life do you need to work on that are preventing you from putting God first?

In what areas are you looking to be prosperous this year?

Let's make prayer a part of your routine. Write or say your prayer of prosperity. Remember prayer is a form of communication with God.

1ST DAY: BIBLE VERSE OF THE DAY: "So you will find favor, and good understanding in the sight of God and man." (Proverbs 3:4).

God wants you to prosper. God wants to bless you. What do you want to achieve this year? What are your specific goals and desires?

What do your goals and desires reveal about your heart?

Take the time to be present with the Lord. Present your goals and desires to God.

2ND DAY: BIBLE VERSE OF THE DAY: "Oh, how abundant is goodness, which you have stored up for those who fear you and worked for those who take refuge in you, in the sight of the children of mankind!" (Psalms 31:19).

What did the Holy Spirit reveal to you in this verse?

3RD DAY: BIBLE VERSE OF THE DAY: "Blessed be the God and Father of our Lord Jesus Christ! According to his great mercy, he has caused us to be born again to a living hope through the resurrection of Jesus Christ from the dead." (1 Peter 1:3).

Let God's word speak to you again. What does this scripture verse say to you? Take a few minutes to close your eyes and meditate.

4TH DAY: BIBLE VERSE OF THE DAY: "The steadfast love of the LORD never ceases; his mercies never come to an end; they are new every morning; great is yourn faithfulness. 'The LORD is my portion,' says my soul, 'therefore I will hope in him.'"
(Lamentations 3:22-24).

Reflect on this Bible verse, what is God trying to teach you?

5TH DAY: BIBLE VERSE OF THE DAY: "Every good gift and every perfect gift is from above, coming down from the Father of lights, with whom there is no variation or shadow due to change." (James 1:17).

God is the source of all good things. We may not notice this when we are going through our trials and tribulations. It is critical to remember that everything we have is a gift from God.

Write or say a prayer in which you thank God for all of His gifts.

Thank you, God, for the gifts you give us through your Spirit. I would like to first thank you for the gift of life.

6TH DAY: BIBLE VERSE OF THE DAY: "This Book of the Law shall not depart from your mouth, but you shall meditate on it day and night, so that you may be careful to do according to all that is written in it. For then you will make your way prosperous, and then you will have good success." (Joshua 1:8).

Our Heavenly Father requires perfect obedience from those of us who trust in Christ Jesus to prosper us in life. When God blesses you, He gives you what you need to be happy and prosperous in life.

Let God's word speak to you today. In what areas of your life do you need to work on being obedient to God?

7TH DAY: BIBLE VERSE OF THE DAY: "May Mercy, peace, and love be multiplied to you.' (Jude 1:2).

What have you learned this week that you want to hold on to?

BENEDICTION: "You shall remember the Lord your God, for it is he who gives you power to get wealth, that he may confirm his covenant that he swore to your fathers, as it is this day." (Deuteronomy 8:18).

WEEK THREE: CLAIM YOUR STOLEN PROPERTIES

Mighty Warrior and My One Defense,

This week I come before you to praise you for your love and your kindness. Thank you for never failing me. How marvelous you are.
The world is a place where there are a lot of trials and tribulations. The power of darkness and violence is everywhere. However, I am not afraid because "no weapon that is formed against me shall prosper." (Isaiah 53:17). With you, "I shatter nations, with you O Lord, I destroy kingdoms." (Jeremiah 51:20). You are a mighty warrior.

It is not Your will for the enemies to steal my inner peace, or my functioning relationships. It is not Your will for the enemies to destroy my business, my livelihood, and my health. It is not Your will for me to give up my dream. Today, I take my stand in your holy name and say to the devil, get thee behind me Satan in the name of Jesus. Please arm me with the battle ax to defend myself and my family. I strongly believe with the sword of the Spirit, I will win. Yes, Yahweh.

This week, I declare victory over my loved ones. I say to the Devil: you are defeated in the powerful name of Jesus. I win the battle today and forever. I pray in the precious name of the Lord Jesus Christ.
Amen

Weekly Reflection

What has the devil stolen from you? It could be your happiness, peace of mind, or ability to forgive and move on. A loving home, a healthy marriage, the ability to have children, a functional relationship with family members, or a good job could be examples too. It could be your ability to provide for yourself and your loved ones. It could be either your physical or mental health. How can you resist the devil and reclaim what he has stolen from you?
Make a claim to God. Write or state what the devil has stolen from you.

It is time for prayer. Concentrate and be present to communicate with Jesus.

Repeat this short prayer below:

Please, Lord, assist me in regaining what I have lost. Allow me to reclaim anything stolen by the devil. Fill my heart with the light of your hope. I pray in the name of Jesus, your son. Amen

1ST DAY: BIBLE VERSE OF THE DAY: "The thief comes only to steal and kill and destroy. I came that they may have life and have it abundantly." (John 10:10).

Has the devil stolen your loved one? Does the person need rescuing from a life of sin? For example, do you have a loved one who is living a life of violence and abuse? Do they need to be set free from physical or mental captivity? Write or say a prayer bringing the person(s) to God.

God, I want You to rescue (list or state the names of the individuals):

2ND DAY: BIBLE VERSE OF THE DAY: "And he told those who sold the pigeons, 'Take these things away; do not make my Father's house a house of trade.'" (John 2:16).

There is hope for everyone in the Atonement of the Lord Jesus Christ. Write or say a prayer for yourself, a person in your life, or a person in your church or community that is struggling with a form of addiction. If you are not sure of any person, you can choose to pray in general for those suffering from addiction.

3RD DAY: BIBLE VERSE OF THE DAY: "The Lord is a man of war, the Lord is His name. Pharaoh's chariots and his host He cast into the sea, and his chosen officers were sunk in the Red Sea. The floods covered them; they went down into the depths like a stone.

Your right hand, O Lord, glorious in power, your right hand, O Lord, shatters the enemy.' (Exodus 15:3-6).

Right now, claim the blood of Jesus to cover you and all your belongings.

4TH DAY: BIBLE VERSE OF THE DAY: "And David inquired of the Lord, 'Shall I pursue after this band? Shall I overtake them?' He answered him, 'Pursue, for you shall surely overtake and shall surely rescue.'" (1 Samuel 30:8).

Today, ask God to give you endurance not to sit quietly but to pursue and overtake in His name.

5TH DAY: BIBLE VERSE OF THE DAY: "He has delivered us from the domain of darkness and transferred us to the kingdom of his beloved Son, 14 in whom we have redemption, the forgiveness of sins." (Colossians 1: 13-14).

When have you overcome a challenge?

What was the challenge?

Write or say a special prayer asking God to keep the devil out of your life and the lives of your loved ones.

6TH DAY: BIBLE VERSE OF THE DAY: "Finally, be strong in the Lord and in the strength of his might. Put on the whole armor of God, that you may be able to stand against the schemes of the devil. For we do not wrestle against flesh and blood, but against the rulers, against the authorities, against the cosmic powers over this present darkness, against the spiritual forces of evil in the heavenly places." (Ephesians 6:10-12).

God says that we can defeat any difficulty or opposition the devil throws at us, whether it be at home, at work, in our community, or anywhere else. We can defeat any difficulty through prayer.

Are you a prayer warrior? A prayer warrior is someone who chooses to fight personal and spiritual battles through prayer and God's wisdom rather than through their own strength. Write or say a prayer asking God to help you be a prayer warrior:

7TH DAY: Take the time to hear God speaking to you. Dedicate at least 15 minutes to God. Remember, there is no formula for hearing God.

After you took the time to hear God, then pray and thank Him for speaking to you.

BENEDICTION: "The blessing of the Lord makes you rich, and he adds no sorrow with it." AMEN. (Proverbs 10:22).

WEEK FOUR: A PRAYER FOR PEACE OF MIND

Sovereign Lord,

The Lion of the tribe of Judas, You are worthy to be praised and honored. I lift up my eyes to you, You O Lord who sits enthroned in heaven.

Now, I desperately need peace of mind. Only You can help me in this situation. I am stressed every day and I cannot concentrate. I feel scared and overwhelmed.
I sometimes have problems sleeping because I am crushed by my worries, doubts, fears, and disillusionments.

In (Philippians 4:6), you said not to worry about tomorrow or be anxious about anything. Today, I want to leave all of my stress on your shoulder, knowing that you are a burden bearer. Your grace is sufficient for me.

Gracious Lord shines your face on my path. Come, take me by your mighty hands. Sustain my feeble faith so that I can be victorious. My victory is your glory. Yahweh, fill my mind with joy and peace and renew my spirit.

I ask all these mercies in the mighty name of Jesus Christ.

Amen.

Weekly Reflection

You might be worried about an upcoming exam at school, a performance review at work, a job interview for a possible new job, bills that haven't been paid, a possible health diagnosis, or even a first date. It is normal to have some worries.

Stress and worry become a problem when it goes on for a long time and gets in the way of your life, which many find hard to handle. It becomes an issue if it affects your relationship with Christ.

(Philippians 4:6) "Do not be anxious about anything, but in everything, by prayer and petition, with thanksgiving, present your requests to God."

What is causing you stress today? You might be worried about what other people think of you, which could be making you feel stressed. Maybe you are stressed about your future, your health, your finances, problems in your relationships, or a loved one.

These and other factors rob us of our peace of mind, and long-term stress can lead to serious health problems.

Did you know that even though you have problems, you can have peace of mind? All your problems don't have to be solved to have peace of mind, but you must be willing to surrender it all to the Lord.

What is stressing you? How has your stress affected or changed your relationship with Christ?

Prayer can alleviate anxiety and provide peace of mind. Make prayer a regular part of your day. Write or say a prayer to God this week, bringing everything that's bothering you or causing you anxiety to His attention.

1ST DAY: BIBLE VERSE OF THE DAY: "Now may the Lord of peace himself give you peace at all times in every way. The Lord be with you all." (2 Thessalonians 3:16).

Create or recite a prayer that asks God to grant you peace of mind.

You can start by saying:

My Father in heaven, I come to you to thank you for all that you have done for me and my family. I am here, God, asking you to grant me peace of mind. You alone are a God of peace.

2ND DAY: BIBLE VERSE OF THE DAY: "Now may the Lord of peace himself give you peace at all times in every way. The Lord be with you all." (1 Thessalonians 3:16).

Take the time to study God's word. What did the Holy Spirit reveal to you in this verse?

3RD DAY: BIBLE VERSE OF THE DAY: "Long life is in her right hand; in her left hand are riches and honor. Her ways are ways of pleasantness, and all her paths are peace." (Proverbs 3:16-17).

Take the time to study God's word. What did the Holy Spirit reveal to you in this verse?

4TH DAY: BIBLE VERSE OF THE DAY: "Peace I leave with you; my peace I give to you. Not as the world gives do I give to you. Let not your hearts be troubled, neither let them be afraid." (John 14:27).

Take the time to study God's word. What promise did Jesus make in this verse? What command did Jesus give in this verse?

5TH DAY: BIBLE VERSE OF THE DAY: "May the God of hope fill you with all joy and peace in believing, so that by the power of the Holy Spirit you may abound in hope." (Romans 15:13).

Pray and reflect on His words:

6TH DAY: BIBLE VERSE OF THE DAY: "May the God of hope fill you with all joy and peace in believing, so that by the power of the Holy Spirit you may abound in hope." (2 Corinthians 13:11).

7TH DAY: Let us proclaim gratitude to the Lamb of God, the Lion of the tribe of Judas for manifold blessings. Take the time to show gratitude to God.

BENEDICTION: "And the peace of God, which surpasses all understanding, will guard your hearts and your minds in Christ Jesus." (Philippians 4:7).

WEEK FIVE:
PRAYER AGAINST INFERTILITY AND BARRENNESS

Glorious Lord, Mighty Savior,

You are the Holy One, I bow down and kneel before you the Maker, the Provider, and the Giver of all things. You deserve all the glory, honor, and praise.

Mighty God, I thank you for giving me a wonderful home, and a great husband.

I thank you for blessing me with three children.

Today, I pray for my friend (family member) who is married and she is struggling to conceive. Your word in (Psalms 127:3, NIV) says that "children are a heritage from the Lord, offspring a reward from Him." This woman hasn't experienced this reward. Please shower her with your blessings. She desires to have a child, but that has not happened. Yahweh, may this season of barrenness wash away and the womb produces fruit.

Jehovah Jireh, you provided for Hannah, you changed her story from childless to childbearing. She desperately needed a child. She went to the temple, knelt, and cried before you. And You showed her your faithfulness in infertility. Please, let her find favor in your eyes like Hannah and Elizabeth. Grant her the desire of her heart.

I pray in the marvelous name of Jesus Christ.

Amen.

Weekly Reflection

We read in the Bible that children are a gift and reward from God. For this reason, many women blame themselves for their inability to have children.

The stigma associated with infertility can result in a variety of emotional problems and feelings, such as guilt, hopelessness, despair, anxiety, and feelings of worthlessness. Due to stigma, numerous couples struggle in private.

You shouldn't blame yourself for your inability to conceive. If you can't have children, you're not being punished for something you did or didn't do. We shouldn't have unfavorable thoughts about a woman or couple battling infertility either.

When a couple has been struggling with infertility for a long time, it can be hard to see how God, who's in charge of everything, could be using their infertility for His glory. Infertility is a test, and God sometimes puts us through trials to see how much faith we have. It can show the genuineness of our faith.

Although for some, infertility is a test from God that will eventually be overcome, for others having children is not part of God's grand design.

This may be a bitter pill to swallow, so you may need to ask for God's assistance in comprehending His plan and decision.

Regardless of the challenges and tribulations you endure, it's critical to trust God and His goodness. Regardless of the difficulties you're facing, God knows when and why He does what He does.

What trial are you currently facing? Are you trusting God in the midst of your trial today? If yes, how are you trusting Him? If not, what can you do to put more of your trust in Him? What have you discovered about yourself as a result of this trial? How did your connection with God develop or grow as you dealt with this particular trial?

What three things you can do to let God be more in charge of your life?

1ST DAY: BIBLE VERSE OF THE DAY: "God has taken away my disgrace." (Genesis 30:23).

Disgrace and embarrassment are emotional setbacks that have the potential to disappoint and lead to low self-esteem. It is extremely unpleasant and has the potentia to destroy your confidence.

In what ways can God remove your shame and disgrace?

Spend some time thinking positively about yourself. Write or say some uplifting things to yourself.

2ND DAY: BIBLE VERSE OF THE DAY: "Therefore the Lord waits to be gracious to you, and therefore he exalts himself to show mercy to you. For the Lord is a God of justice; blessed are all those who wait for him." (Isaiah 30:18).

In the Bible, the idea of wrongdoing includes treating others unfairly, abusing them, and being violent among many other things. The God of justice wants to restore justice. What justice do you want the ultimate judge to do for you? Bring all of the injustices to God in prayer. It might be injustice in your home, at work, community, or in your city.

3RD DAY: BIBLE VERSE OF THE DAY: "And now I commend you to God and to the word of his grace, which is able to build you up and to give you the inheritance among all those who are sanctified." (Acts 20:32).

Paul used these phrases: "I command you, build you up, and give the inheritance."

What do Paul's words and phrases say and mean to you?

How does God's word give you strength when you are weak and peace when you are afraid?

4TH DAY: BIBLE VERSE OF THE DAY: "I will greatly rejoice in the Lord my soul shall exult in my God, for he has clothed me with the garments of salvation; he has covered me with the robe of righteousness, as a bridegroom decks himself like a priest with a beautiful headdress, and as a bride adorns herself with her jewels." (Isaiah 61:10).

God clothed us with the garment of salvation as a bridegroom. He provided us with this very costly garment and dressed us up because He thinks highly of us. You can now make a promise to God and get that beautiful garment of salvation. What does your garment of salvation look like? Describe what your garment looks like.

5TH DAY: BIBLE VERSE OF THE DAY: "He gives the barren woman a home, making her the joyous mother of children. Praise the Lord!" (Psalms 113:9).

We cannot accomplish things with our own strength or power. The Bible asserts that God is the All-Powerful, and the Supreme Being. As a Christian, how can you find God's power?

How is God's mighty power at work in your life and your household?

What can you do daily to experience God's power?

6TH DAY: BIBLE VERSE OF THE DAY: "First of all, then, I urge that supplications, prayers, intercessions, and thanksgivings be made for all people." (1 Timothy 2:1). Christians are expected to pray not only for themselves, but for all people. Do you have an intimate relationship with Christ through prayer? As Christians, we want to have an intimate relationship with Christ. Intimacy is defined as closeness to others, and this type of closeness is desired by many.

What does it mean to have an intimate relationship with God?

How can you develop a close relationship with the almighty God?

Take five minutes and simply enjoy a time of intimacy and solitude with God.

7TH DAY: Give the Maker the highest praise for all the prayers answered.

BENEDICTION: "The Lord bless you and keep you; the Lord make his face shine upon you and be gracious to you; The Lord lift up his countenance upon you and give you peace." (Numbers 6: 24).

WEEK SIX: A PRAYER TO COPE WITH DIVORCE

Loving Heavenly Father,

I lift my eyes to You for help. I know my help will come from You, the Maker of heaven and earth.
I come to you to bring my family to you who is full of pain, sadness, bitterness, and confusion. Her heart is torn to pieces. Her husband has left her. She already feels the burden of loneliness as the head of the household.

When she entered this marriage, she expected it to last until death. Unfortunately, he decided against her wishes to divorce her.
Right now, she feels so alone and sad. It is very hard for her.
She complained that she can't focus, and it is very difficult to get through her daily routine and stay productive.

Lord, she needs healing. As it is written in Your word in (Psalms 147:3):
"He heals the broken-hearted and binds up their wounds." Please Holy Father, heal her wounds, which are stress, guilt, and doubt. Touch her mind, spirit, and soul and remove lingering doubt that makes her feel guilty. Help her in understanding that she is beautiful, valuable, fearfully, and wonderfully made in your likeness.

Help her to replace fear with faith. As your word teaches (1Peter 5:7) "Cast all your anxiety on him because he cares for us." I pray in the most powerful name of Jesus. Amen.

Weekly Reflection

Sometimes, a broken relationship is extremely difficult to accept. It is extremely painful and taxing. It can affect us in numerous ways, including our hearts, relationships, and finances. It needs not to disturb our tranquility and happiness. Remember that God always has a plan for our lives, and we must have faith in Him. God loves you regardless of your marital or relationship status, relationship sins, or failures. What do you fear most in terms of relationships? What new qualities have you discovered about yourself after experiencing a loss? What are the most significant life changes and obstacles you've encountered thus far?

1ST DAY: BIBLE VERSE OF THE DAY: "And after you have suffered a little while, the God of all grace, who has called you to his eternal glory in Christ, will himself restore, confirm, strengthen, and establish you." (1 Peter 5: 10).

What do you think it means that the God of all grace will restore, confirm, strengthen and establish you?

2ND DAY: BIBLE VERSE OF THE DAY: "Why are you cast down, O my soul, and why are you in turmoil within me? Hope in God; for I shall again praise him, my salvation and my God." (Psalm 43:5).

What is hope? Hope is the desire for something wonderful to happen in the future.

Here are some questions to consider:

How can we have hope in this world of uncertainty when everything appears to be hopeless?

How can you find true hope in the Lord?

What do you hope to achieve by the end of the year?

What are your hopes for your family, children, home, and marriage?

3RD DAY: BIBLE VERSE OF THE DAY: "Peace I leave with you; my peace I give to you. Not as the world gives do I give to you. Let not your hearts be troubled, neither let them be afraid." (John 14:27).

In a world of chaos and insecurity, we desperately need God's peace to calm us. Does the peace of God imply that our lives will be devoid of significant obstacles?

What exactly is the peace of God?

How can you attain this supernatural calm?

How can you maintain God's peace in your heart and mind?

4TH DAY: BIBLE VERSE OF THE DAY: "For his anger is but for a moment, and his favor is for a lifetime. Weeping may tarry for the night, but joy comes with the morning." (Psalms 30:5).

The Bible says, "Weeping may tarry for the night." How long might a night be? The answer depends on how long you hold your anger. The longer you keep the anger. The longer the duration of the night will last. If you wish the morning to have joy, don't dwell in darkness but let God's power transform you. What does it really mean that joy comes in the morning?

5TH DAY: BIBLE VERSE OF THE DAY: "They will fight against you, but they shall not prevail against you, for I am with you, declares the Lord, to deliver you." (Jeremiah 1:19). This verse provides the reassuring knowledge that your enemies will fight against you, but they will not prevail because God is with you.

Whoever stands with God will prevail, as He has promised us His strength. God is with you no matter how difficult the battle may be. What experience in your past made you more aware of God's assurance?

6TH DAY: BIBLE VERSE OF THE DAY: "For I know the plans I have for you,' declares the Lord, 'plan for welfare and not for evil, to give you a future and a hope.'" (Jeremiah 29:11).

God's plan for you is a great plan to give hope and a future. However, remember that it is up to you to discover what this plan is.

What do you believe God's plan should entail?

What does your personal relationship with the Lord look like?

Can you recall a time when you desired control over a situation but felt that it was out of your hands?

Did you realize it was in God's will for your life?

What can you do today to relinquish control and allow God to direct your life?

7TH DAY: Give the Maker the highest praise for all the prayers answered.

BENEDICTION: "The grace of the Lord Jesus Christ be with your Spirit." (Philippians 4:23).

WEEK SEVEN: GOD OF MULTIPLICATION

Eternal Father, the Miracle-Working God,

I came before you as a child coming to his dad seeking assistance. Your word in (Matthew 7:8) tells me that everyone who asks, receives. So, now I ask you to perform a miracle of multiplication for me and my family.

Yes, Yahweh, you have done it several times in history. You multiplied and met the needs of the five thousand and four thousand individuals. I beg you to do it again for me with my finances. Only you can help in this distress. I cannot generate enough funds to fulfill my financial obligation. My financial resources are extremely limited, and my needs are substantial.

You are the good shepherd who says your children won't lack anything. Please help me to find a way to meet my needs. So, I patiently wait for you. I pray in the wonderful name of Jesus Christ my Savior.
Amen.

Weekly Reflection

You need to know that God is at work in your life regardless of how much money you have. It is understood that having sufficient funds to meet your needs is important, as we require money to pay for the things that make life possible. God has the ability to transform your current financial situation into something wonderful.

Do you believe that God has already established a wealth system for His children that cannot fail?

Are you able to see your financial struggle as an opportunity to trust in God?

Do you see it as an opportunity to place your sole confidence in Him?

How would you describe your current financial situation?

What is your current relationship with money?

How do you manage your finances?

Is there something you can do to better manage your finances?

What resources are available to you to help you manage your finances better?

Have you brought your finances to God?

How can you trust God with your finances?

How can you honor God with your finances?

God owns everything on earth, and He entrusted you and me with everything we possess. And we are just stewards. In (Deuteronomy 8:18), God said, "You shall remember the Lord your God, for it is he who gives you power to get wealth, that he may confirm his covenant that he swore to your fathers, as it is this day."

God reminded the nation that He alone possesses the ability, power, and strength to produce wealth.

Does the Bible state that God will make you wealthy? Or does it state that He will give you the ability to generate wealth? If you are unsure, take some time to read and meditate on (Deuteronomy 8:18) again. Begin to pray and claim the power so that everything you touch or do will produce wealth for you.

1ST DAY: BIBLE VERSE OF THE DAY: "Give her of the fruit of her hands, and let her works praise her in the gates." (Proverbs 31:25).

What does this Bible verse reveal to you?

2ND DAY: BIBLE VERSE OF THE DAY: "The silver is mine, and the gold is mine, says Yahweh of Hosts." (Haggai 2:8).

God created and owns all of God's resources. You may encounter extremely challenging conditions in your life, and while serving God. This passage encourages us to put our faith in God even in the midst of adversity and difficulty.

What holds you back from devoting every aspect of your life to God?

3RD DAY: BIBLE VERSE OF THE DAY: "And my God will supply every need of yours according to his riches in glory in Christ Jesus." (Philippians 4:19).

This verse offers a promise that God would never abandon those who seek Him. He will provide for our physical, material, and spiritual needs.

This verse describes God's desire to reward us for our efforts. What is your good work for God? Do you feel obligated to work for God as His faithful servant?

How can you accomplish God's work in your community?

How do you envision your role in God's service?

What do you believe may impede your ministry to God?

Close your eyes for a moment and pray that God will use you for His kingdom and help you to have a fruitful ministry.

4TH DAY: BIBLE VERSE OF THE DAY: "You shall remember the Lord your God, for it is he who gives you power to get wealth, that he may confirm his covenant that he swore to your fathers, as it is this day." (Deuteronomy 8:18).

Let God's word speak to you now. Silence everything around you, be still, and meditate. What did the Holy Spirit reveal to you?

5TH DAY: BIBLE VERSE OF THE DAY: "In all toil there is profit, but mere talk tends only to poverty." (Proverbs 14:23).

The concept of labor originated with God, who created everything. Money is generally compensation for labor. And as a business owner, success involves time and work. Money does not materialize out of just anywhere.

Take a moment to pray for the success of your endeavors and the fulfillment of your work.

6TH DAY: BIBLE VERSE OF THE DAY: "Out of them shall come songs of thanksgiving, and the voices of those who celebrate. I will multiply them, and they shall not be few, I will make them honored, and they shall not be small." (Jeremiah 30:19).

Are you prepared enough so that God can multiply your affairs in quantity and quality?

This is the promise God gave to Jeremiah.

Right now, pray and ask God to open your spiritual eyes to see the opportunities that are available for you.

7TH DAY: Say a prayer of thanksgiving and praise for all the blessings without measure.

BENEDICTION: "The Lord bless you and keep you; the Lord make his face shine upon you and be gracious to you; The Lord lifts up his countenance upon you and gives you peace." (Numbers 6:2).

WEEK EIGHT: MIGHTY HEALER

Jehovah Rapha, the Great and Mighty Healer,

I bow down before you and confess my sin. You are a great physician and I need healing because I am both physically and spiritually unwell.
Your word declares that my body is the temple of the Holy Spirit, but I know that diseases cannot cohabit with the Holy Spirit.

You have healed many in the past. Naaman was one among those cured of leprosy by dipping himself in the River Jordan seven times.

Please, Yahweh, free me from my illness. Heal my wound, or whatever troubles my body. Today, I declare all the chains of sickness fallen off of me in the name of Jesus. Spirit of infirmity, in the name of Jesus, I cast you out of me. I cast the spirit of hypertension out of me. As your words declare, "by your wounds, we are healed" (Isaiah 53:5).
Thank you for healing my body. I pray in the powerful name of Jesus, my Savior and King.
Amen.

Weekly Reflection

It is critical to speak healing, courage, and faith over your body, friends, and family. God is a powerful healer. According to the Bible, Jesus is the Great Physician, the healer of both the body and soul. When we are unwell, we all pray to God for a healing miracle. The name Jehovah Rapha means "to heal, cure, restore, or make whole."

Write or say a prayer, using the name of Jehovah Rapha to heal you or a loved one.

1ST DAY: BIBLE VERSE OF THE DAY: "He has delivered us from the domain of darkness and transferred us to the kingdom of his beloved Son, in whom we have redemption, the forgiveness of sins." (Colossians 1:13-14).

What are your thoughts about the verse, what does God reveal through His Word?

2ND DAY: BIBLE VERSE OF THE DAY: "Therefore, confess your sins to one another and pray for one another, that you may be healed. The prayer of a righteous person has great power as it is working." (James 5:16).

God required us to pray for one another in order to overcome our individual sins and remain spiritually uplifted.

Are you a member of a church family, or do you know a group of Christians from whom you can seek support and prayer?

Do you know a Christian for whom you can pray due to bodily, mental, or spiritual illness? God is attentive and receptive.

Write or recite a prayer for another person for their physical, mental, or spiritual recovery.

3RD DAY: BIBLE VERSE OF THE DAY: "But Jesus on hearing this answered him, "Do not fear; only believe, and she will be well." (Luke 8:50).

According to this Bible text, what are the benefits of obeying God's commands?

4TH DAY: BIBLE VERSE OF THE DAY: "Saying, 'If you will diligently listen to the voice of the Lord your God, and do that which is right in his eyes, and give ear to his commandments and keep all his statutes, I will put none of the diseases on you that I put on the Egyptians, for I am the Lord, your healer.'" (Exodus 15:26).

God is the greatest healer. You can cast your burdens at His feet. The grace of God is sufficient. Do you rely on God's grace? Do you keep God's commandments and believe that God will look after you regardless of your illness, whether physical, mental, or spiritual? Spend some time praying to God for healing in your life.

5TH DAY: BIBLE VERSE OF THE DAY: "The Lord opens the eyes of the blind. The Lord lifts up those who are bowed down; the Lord loves the righteous. The Lord watches over the sojourners; he upholds the widow and the fatherless, but the way of the wicked he brings to ruin." (Psalm 146:8-9).

Jesus approached the blind man and asked him what he desired. "I want to receive my sight," he said (Mark 10:51). Jesus addresses you personally. Do you hear Him speak? Take a few moments to be silent in front of the Lord and listen to what He has to say to you. Do you want your health to be restored? Do you hear God's voice speaking to you?

What do you want Jesus to do for you? Are you looking for physical, emotional, or spiritual healing? Tell God exactly what you want to be healed of.

6TH DAY: BIBLE VERSE OF THE DAY: "You shall serve the Lord your God, and he will bless your bread and your water, and I will take sickness away from among you." (Exodus 23:25).

Most of us on the planet need some form of healing.

Some people need healing for physical illnesses, while others need healing from trauma caused by something that happened to them as a child, an adolescent, or an adult. Others require healing as a result of the loss of a loved one.
It is critical to pray for the healing of yourself, your family, and your loved ones.

Write or say a prayer for yourself and others.

7TH DAY: Prayer of Thanks and Praise for Prayers Answered.

BENEDICTION: "The Lord bless you and keep you; the Lord makes his face shine upon you and be gracious to you; The Lord lifts up his countenance upon you and gives you peace." (Numbers 6:24).

WEEK NINE: TODAY IS THE DAY OF DECISION

Eternal Father,

As I approach your throne of grace, I thank you for creating this new day.

Please help me not to be distracted, diluted, frustrated, or disappointed today. Help me to always look forward to a bright tomorrow, believing that you will take care of everything on this day that you have made and that all things will work for my good.

Today, Lord, you set before me life and death. Help me to always choose life, oh God.

Lord, guide me today in making wise decisions, carefully selecting the people in my life, and rejecting any negative thoughts that enter my mind.

Oh Holy God, help me to recognize that I am beautiful, intelligent, and wanted. Your grace is sufficient for me, God. I cannot make it on my own but I can do everything because you are my strength.

Please, let me know that I am your choice. Yahweh, guide me today to find my heart's desire and solutions to my problems. Today, my father assist me in refusing any kind of abuse from those who only want to harm me. Today, guarantee me your strength, your healing, and your comfort. Today, baptize me again with the Holy Spirit.

Lord, anoint me. Lord, I come asking that you heal those around me with broken hearts, relieve those that feel oppressed, and ease the suffering of the outcasts.

Today, Lord, help me to be optimistic and listen to your voice.

Please help me to recognize the thoughts that are not helpful to me. Allow only Your words to enter my mind and thoughts.

In Jesus Christ's most precious name.

Amen.

Weekly Reflection

Do you appreciate and cherish the life God has given you?

Do you know who God created you to be and rejoice in that?

I hope you know that you are loved. Are you having difficulty loving yourself?

Are you having negative thoughts, or feeling like you don't have much worth?

We are all sinners who have done some things we are not proud of. God does not want us to spend our lives thinking negatively about ourselves or feeling worthless. God loves you and has a high value on your life. He wants you to remember that you are the most important thing to Him. He wants you to dedicate your life fully to Him.

Well, today is the day.

God wants you to embrace this day and make a decision to serve Him.

You can choose to serve God.

Have you dedicated your life to serving God?

What are some ways you can serve God at home, work, or in your community?

1ST DAY: BIBLE VERSE OF THE DAY: "This is the day that the Lord has made; let us rejoice and be glad in it." (Psalm 118:24).

What are you most thankful for today?

2ND DAY: BIBLE VERSE OF THE DAY: "Trust in the Lord with all your heart, and do not lean on your own understanding. In all your ways acknowledge him, and he will make straight your paths." (Proverb 3:5-6).

God's promise in this verse shows that He will direct your steps. What decision do you need to make in the near future? Have you prayed about your choice? Do you find it difficult to put your trust in God when making a decision? When was the last time you went to God about a major decision?

Write or say a prayer asking God to assist you with this upcoming decision in your life.

3RD DAY: BIBLE VERSE OF THE DAY: "And we know that for those who love God all things work together for good, for those who are called according to his purpose." (Romans 8:28).

Today, abundant grace is available for you and your family. What has God's abundant grace brought you through? Write or say a prayer thanking God for His abundant grace.

4TH DAY: BIBLE VERSE OF THE DAY: "For I command you today to love the Lord your God, to walk in obedience to him, and to keep his commands, decrees and laws; then you will live and increase, and the Lord your God will bless you in the land you are entering to possess." (Deuteronomy 30:16).

What is your desire today? Are you following God's commandment?

5TH DAY: BIBLE VERSE OF THE DAY: "Finally, brothers and sisters, whatever is true, whatever is noble, whatever is right, whatever is pure, whatever is lovely, whatever is admirable if anything is excellent or praiseworthy—think about such things." (Philippians 4:8).

Allow the words of God to speak to you through this verse. Consider the points made by Paul, what advice is he sharing with you?

6TH DAY: BIBLE VERSE OF THE DAY: "He has made everything beautiful in its time. Also, he has put eternity into man's heart, yet so that he cannot find out what God has done from the beginning to the end." (Ecclesiastes 3:11).

God's creation is beautiful, and everything occurs precisely when it should.
You are a part of God's beautiful creation and God has a plan for your life. Sometimes, we might have a hard time understanding why, but it allows us to trust Him, which is God's ultimate objective.

Do you trust in God's plan? What can you do today that will allow you to surrender to God's plan?

7TH DAY: Today is a Declaration to God's Day.
Repeat the following: "Lord, I declare the word of life, word of success, and word of favor on my life today."

BENEDICTION: "May he grant you your heart's desire, and fulfill all your plans!" (Psalm 20:4).

WEEK TEN: A DAUGHTER'S PRAYER FOR HER MOTHER

Father God in Heaven,

I join with a multitude of heavenly hosts at this moment to praise and glorify your holy name. The creator of Heaven and Earth. Before the mountain was created, you created the world, and from eternity to eternity, You are God.

You have blessed me with a wonderful mother. I come to you because her health is critical. I need a breakthrough in her life. I asked that you heal her like you healed the woman in the Bible who was crippled for 18 years. What you have done for this woman, you are able to do that and much more for my mother.

Jesus, you are the Great Healer. Please, heal my mother. Her strength needs to be restored. Please provide comfort to my mom as she has comforted me over the years.

Your word declares: "And the LORD will take away from you all sickness, and none of the evil diseases of Egypt, which you knew, will he inflict on you, but he will lay them on all who hate you" (Deuteronomy 7:15). May your favor be upon your servant.
I pray in the marvelous name of Jesus Christ, the King of kings and Lord of lords.

Amen.

Weekly Reflection

A mother is a role model, nurturer, source of strength, and comfort for her daughter. When we come into the world, our first connection is often with our mother.

Our mother is often the first person we bond with. Some of us have had great and healthy relationships with our mothers, but for others, our relationships were complex or dysfunctional.

As we become mature, our relationship changes throughout the years, and if you have had a loving relationship, your feelings for one another remain the same.

How would you describe your mother? What was the best or most useful thing your mother taught you that you hope to pass on to the next generation?

What kind of relationship do you have with your mother? How do you think your relationship with your mother made you the woman you are today? There is a special gift that you as a daughter can give to your mother. It is the gift of prayer.

At this point, you can choose to pray for your mother, a mother figure, a mentor, or a loved one. You can pray that your mother may have physical, emotional, or spiritual healing. It is up to you. If you did not have an ideal relationship with your mother, you can choose to ask God to heal your broken relationship.

Speak the word of favor and grace now on your mother in the name of Jesus.

1ST DAY: BIBLE VERSE OF THE DAY: "We ought always to give thanks to God for you, brothers, as is right, because your faith is growing abundantly, and the love of every one of you for one another is increasing." (2 Thessalonians 1:3).

How do you interpret this Scripture verse?
"Your faith is growing abundantly" describes a relationship with God that continues to grow stronger and deeper.

At this point in your life, can you say that your faith in God is growing?

Do you have a strong faith in Jesus Christ, our Lord? What factors do you believe influence your faith?

Take a moment to thank your God for the faith you have now and ask Him to help you have a stronger faith in Him.

2ND DAY: BIBLE VERSE OF THE DAY: "He himself bore our sins in his body on the tree, that we might die to sin and live to righteousness. By his wounds you have been healed." (1 Peter 2:24).

Let God's word speak to you today. What does it mean that Jesus bore your sins?
How did Jesus Christ's wounds free you from the penalty of sin?

3RD DAY: BIBLE VERSE OF THE DAY: "And these signs will accompany those who believe in my name they will cast out demons; they will speak in new tongues;

they will pick up serpents with their hands, and if they drink any deadly poison, it will not hurt them, they will lay their hands on the sick, and they will recover."
(Mark 16:17-18).

Satan is the source of all evil in the world, including death, sickness, various forms of abuse, and demonic oppression.

You can combat the devil by speaking God's word. Write or say a prayer asking God to give you strength to combat the enemy.

4TH DAY: BIBLE VERSE OF THE DAY: "He gives power to the faint, and to him who has no might he increases strength." (Isaiah 40:29).

Are you becoming weary of your faith? Are you feeling disconnected from God? What do you think you can do today to connect better with God?

Let us spend a few moments listening to the Lord. What does God's word say to you today? Write or say a prayer asking the Divine Helper to strengthen your faith and give you power.

5TH DAY: BIBLE VERSE OF THE DAY: "He sent out his word and healed them, and delivered them from their destruction. Let them thank the LORD for his steadfast love, for his wondrous works to the children of man!" (Psalm 107:20-21).

What did the Holy Spirit reveal to you in this verse?

6TH DAY: BIBLE VERSE OF THE DAY: "Many are the afflictions of the righteous, but the Lord delivers him out of them all." (Psalm 34:19).

Allow God's words to speak to you today. As Christians, we are not immune to pain, illness, or suffering. As Christians, we can trust God to deliver us from our trials.

His deliverance can be both specific and physical. At times, it may be to give you the strength you need to get through your trial. What trials has God delivered you from or given you the strength to endure?

7TH DAY: Give the Lord your highest praise for His excellent greatness! Praise Him for a wonderful week.

BENEDICTION: "The LORD bless you and keep you; the LORD make his face to shine upon you and be gracious to you; the LORD lift up his countenance upon you and give you peace." (Numbers 6:24-26).

WEEK ELEVEN: GOD'S PROMISE WILL NEVER RETURN TO VOID

Merciful Father,

You are my Rock and my Hope. Thank you for keeping your promises to me. Your word says, "Whatever I ask in your name, I will receive it." Today, I come to you because I want to sign a contract with you and seal it with the amazing promise of "declare and decree". I am confident that Your Words will never be void. Your Words will produce results, and miracles will occur.

Your promises are a big encouragement for me to abide by Your Word. Today, Lord, I declare and decree in Your Holy name, and so will it be. I declare that You will go before me today and make difficult situations easier for me and my family.

I know, Yahweh, that you already have the right people in place, the right opportunities, and the right solutions to the problems I don't yet have. Nobody, no disease, and no disappointment can derail your plan for me, God. You always deliver on your promises.In Jesus's name, I declare that my loved ones will be saved and will serve you as their Savior.

I declare in the name of Jesus that my loved ones will be healed physically or mentally. You were wounded for our transgressions, broken for our sins. We are healed because of your stripes. Thank you, Lord, for saving and healing your servants. Lord, my final proclamation for the day is that it is not too late for me to fulfill all of Your plans for me.

I know you're preparing me right now, Lord, because you're about to shower me with unlimited grace to help me realize my dreams. With your power, Lord, I can work diligently and fulfill your plans for me.

Righteous God, I believe this is my moment, Lord.

I am grateful for the promise that your goodness and mercy will accompany me every day of my life. I pray in the wonderful names of the Father, Son, and Holy Spirit.

Amen.

What are your plans for the day? How do you approach your daily planning? Is it in a holistic manner? What are your plans for the coming week? What are your plans for the coming month and year? What are your long-term plans for your life? God desires that you make plans for your life. He wants you to plan for your family, your marriage, your finances, your education, and your career among many other things.

Have you ever made plans that didn't work out and you felt defeated in life as a result? Consider it for a moment. What was one of your plans that did not work out? Were you the mastermind behind this plan? Did you consult God about your plan at any time?

God is capable of carrying out whatever He intends in your plans. I want to encourage you to seek God's wisdom and guidance in your plans throughout your life. If you speak God's word over all your plans, it will not go unnoticed by Him. Today, I want you to believe this truth: "So shall my word be that goes out from my mouth it shall not return to me empty, but it shall accomplish that which I purpose and shall succeed in the thing for which I sent it." (Isaiah 55:11).

When we proclaim God's Word, we can be confident that it will do its work and impact the lives of those who hear it. Speak God's Word over your church, family, marriage, career, business, finances, unsaved friends, family members, and coworkers. The world should know that God's Word is powerful, active, quick, and alive. Write or say a prayer thanking God for His promises and ask Him to direct you and be part of your life.

1ST DAY: BIBLE VERSE OF THE DAY: "Delight yourself in the LORD, and he will give you the desires of your heart." (Psalm 37:4).

What does this Bible verse symbolize to you?

2ND DAY: BIBLE VERSE OF THE DAY: "Now to him who is able to do far more abundantly than all that we ask or think, according to the power at work within us." (Ephesians 3:20).

Take the time to study God's Word. What did the Holy Spirit reveal to you in this verse?

3RD DAY: BIBLE VERSE OF THE DAY: "Blessed is the man who walks not in the counse of the wicked, nor stands in the way of sinners, nor sits in the seat of scoffers; but his delight is in the law of the LORD, and on his law he meditates day and night. He is like a tree planted by streams of water that yields its fruit in its season, and its leaf does not wither. In all that he does, he prospers." (Psalm 1:1-3).

Close your eyes for a few minutes and stay focused on Jesus for a moment.

4TH DAY: VERSE OF THE DAY: "And this is the confidence that we have toward him, that if we ask anything according to his will he hears us." (1 John 5:14).

When we pray, we should do so with full assurance in the answers we will receive from God. We are to put our trust in His Word and not in our own understanding. Write or say a prayer to God asking Him to help us learn to put our trust in Him.

5TH DAY: BIBLE VERSE OF THE DAY: "Truly, I say to you whoever says to this mountain, 'Be taken up and thrown into the sea,' and does not doubt his heart, but believes that what he says will come to pass, it will be done for him. Therefore, I tell you, whatever you ask in prayer, believe that you have received it, and it will be yours." (Mark 11:23-24).

What does this Bible verse say about God?

6TH DAY: BIBLE VERSE OF THE DAY: "Commit your work to the LORD, and your plans will be established." (Proverbs 16:3).

Have you entrusted God with your daily, weekly, monthly, and yearly plans? Have you considered prioritizing God's will over yours?

Write or say a prayer asking God to help you rely on Him and to prioritize His will over yours.

God, I am trusting you to:

7TH DAY: Write or say a prayer of thanksgiving for prayers answered.

BENEDICTION: "And the peace of God, which surpasses all understanding, will guard your hearts and your minds in Christ Jesus." (Philippians 4:7).

WEEK TWELVE: GET BACK UP AGAIN

Sovereign Lord!

The God of the universe, You deserve all the honor and glory because you are the only God. Thank you for your promise that never fails.

You know life is full of chaos that pushes us down. They are setbacks, devil temptation, discouragement, doubts, and the wrong things that are not pleasing to you.

We are sorry Lord.

At times, we fell down, and couldn't get back up. But your Word teaches, "the right fall seven times they rise again." So, please help us to get back up again.

You reinstated Peter after he denied you three times.

As I pray this prayer, Lord, help me to refuse to stay down there. Lord, help me to reject addiction, anger, and jealousy, and take a determination to continue moving forward.

I'm sure no challenge is too difficult for You. There is no temptation You cannot overcome, no sin You cannot forgive, and no life you cannot restore. You can do it for me, my family, and my friends as you help Samson get back up again.

I ask all these mercies in the name of the Most High God.

Amen.

Have you ever fallen and struggled to get up after injuring your leg or feet? Perhaps you attempted to get up before anyone noticed you.

Have you ever hit rock bottom in terms of finances, emotions, or morals and seen no way out? You may be experiencing or have recently experienced a major slump and might feel ashamed as a result. You can't see the light because of the fog above you, and you might feel like you're drowning. You might be wondering if these issues are a result of your past transgressions.

What about your spiritual life? Have you ever experienced a spiritual low? Reflect on a time when you fell down and struggled to get up. Did you talk to God about this situation?

Were you able to move on from that particular period in your life?

Do you still feel like you're down and haven't gotten back up? Regardless of where we are, our mistakes, errors, faulty ways, or current situations, Jesus loves us. He died to atone for our sins. Whatever our current situation or whatever is causing us to feel down, Jesus is bigger than it. Don't stay down! It's time for you to get back up again! You may have been or are currently down, but that does not mean you will remain so. Remember that sin is sin, and there is no such thing as a small or big sin. The word of God says, "for though the righteous fall seven times, they rise again, but the wicked stumble when calamity strikes" (Proverbs 24:16 NIV). Please hang in there. You will get up again. Nobody ever falls so low they can't get back up with the Lord. So, if you repent, decide to have a personal relationship with Him, and actively pursue righteousness in your life. God will restore you. Take a moment to connect with God because He is not done with you yet. Free yourself of your past and rise again.

Write or say a prayer and ask Jesus to help you get back up and use you for His glory.

1ST DAY: BIBLE VERSE OF THE DAY: "For God so loved the world, that he gave his only Son, that whoever believes in him should not perish but have eternal life." (John 3:16). Today, how can you worship God in light of this verse?

2ND DAY: BIBLE VERSE OF THE DAY: "We are afflicted in every way, but not crushed; perplexed, but not driven to despair, persecuted, but not forsaken; struck down, but destroyed." (2 Corinthians 4:8-9).

Now, take a deep breath, close your eyes and picture God on His throne. What do you envision?

3RD DAY: BIBLE VERSE OF THE DAY: "But He said to me, 'My grace is sufficient for you, for my power is made perfect in weakness.' Therefore, I will boast all the more gladly of my weakness, so that the power of Christ may rest upon me." (2 Corinthians 12:9). How does this Bible verse help you get closer to God?

4TH DAY: BIBLE VERSE OF THE DAY: "Remain in Me, as I also remain in you. No branch can bear fruit by itself; it must remain in the vine. Neither can you bear fruit unless you remain in me? 'I am the vine; you are the branches. If you remain in me and I in you, you will bear much fruit; apart from me you can do nothing.'" (John 15:4-5).

Take note of what these verses have to say. What changes does God want to make in your life as a result of the verses you just read?

5TH DAY: BIBLE VERSE OF THE DAY: "Behold, I stand at the door and knock. If anyone hears my voice and opens the door, I will come in to him and eat with him, and he with me." (Revelation 3:20).

What is God trying to teach you through this Bible verse?

6TH DAY: BIBLE VERSE OF THE DAY: "No, in all these things we are more than conquerors through him who loved us." (Romans 8:37).

Let God's Word speak to you now. Silence everything around you, be still, and meditate.

What did the Holy Spirit reveal to you?

7TH DAY: Prayer of praise and thanksgiving for prayers answered.

BENEDICTION: "The Lord bless you and keep you; the Lord make his face shine upon you and be gracious to you; The Lord lift up his countenance upon you and give you peace." (Numbers 6:24)

WEEK THIRTEEN: PRAY MORE AND WORRY LESS

Dear God, Heavenly Father,

How great and how awesome you are. I glorify your holy name for what you have done and for what you are doing in my life. I am so very grateful for your grace and the blessings that you lavished upon me every day.

I pray for assistance in order to avoid worrying about things outside of my control. Help me in mastering my life and not allow my negative beliefs to influence my behavior. I am determined to overcome the doubt that impedes my daily life. Blessed Redeemer, assist me in disassociating from all toxic minds that may cause confusion on my path. Please, release me from all of this.

You are my Rock and my refuge. You say I am more than a conqueror and I'm choosing to believe that in faith. I need Your victory in my situation. I can't see my way out, so I beg that you free me. Your Word says, "do not be anxious about anything, but in every situation, by prayer and petition, thanksgiving, present your request" (Philippians 4:6). So, right now, I present my request, and I know with you there is victory. I ask all these mercies in the wonderful name of Jesus.

Amen.

Many people nowadays worry about everything, including the future, the past, and the present. We are constantly worried, even among God's children, and some choose to do a variety of things to deal with their worries.

We manage to try a variety of things to help us cope with our worries rather than using the most powerful tool we have: prayer. The Bible says that we should not worry about anything but rather pray about everything.

At this point in your life, what are you concerned about? It can be work, family, marriage, children, grandchildren, finance, church, community, or your country.

Do you believe that worrying will solve your problem or the problem of the world?

What can you do as a believer to combat the spirit of anxiety?

What are your thoughts on Paul's advice to not "worry about anything; instead, pray about everything"?

As Jesus said in (Matthew 6:27), "And which of you by being anxious can add a single hour to his span of life?"

Only the power of prayer can help you overcome all of your worries and anxieties.

The only thing you can do is put your faith in God's promises.

God is the Giver and the Sustainer. In the wilderness, He provided for the Israelites.

He loves us so much that He sent His Son to die for our sins. How could He not be concerned about us?

"Do not be anxious about anything, but in every situation, by prayer and petition, with thanksgiving, present your requests to God." (Philippians 4:6 NIV).

Write or say a prayer thanking God for His Grace and requesting that He assist you in trusting Him with your problems.

1ST DAY: BIBLE VERSE OF THE DAY: "I can do all things through him who strengthens me." (Philippians 4:13).

Although life can be difficult at times, God is always with you.

Consider a difficult experience in your life where you knew God was with you. Write or say a prayer of thanksgiving to our Heavenly father.

2ND DAY: BIBLE VERSE OF THE DAY: "But let him ask in faith, with no doubting, for one who doubts is like a wave of the sea that is driven and tossed by the wind." (James 1:6). In light of this verse, how can you worship God today?

3RD DAY: BIBLE VERSE OF THE DAY: "Trust in the Lord with all your heart, and do not lean on your own understanding." (Proverbs 3:5).

What does the concept of trust mean to you?

When you trust someone, you believe in them, rely on them, and have complete faith in them. Do you believe in God? Do you have complete faith in Him?

4TH DAY: VERSE OF THE DAY: "Let us then with confidence draw near to the throne of grace, that we may receive mercy and find grace to help in time of need."

(Hebrews 4:16).

Let God's Word speak to you now. Silence everything around you, be still, and meditate.

What did the Holy Spirit reveal to you?

5TH DAY: VERSE OF THE DAY: "In my distress, I called upon the Lord; to my God, I cried for help. From his temple he heard my voice, and my cry to him reached his ears."

(Psalm 18:6).

Over and over again, the Bible tells us that God loves us and always does what He says He will do. Do you have any problems that are making you unhappy and causing you distress at this point in your life?

What do you think God is trying to accomplish through and with you during this difficult time?

Have you decided to place your faith in God as you go through life?

6TH DAY: BIBLE VERSE OF THE DAY: "But when you pray, go into your room and shut the door and pray to your Father who is in secret. And your Father who sees in secret will reward you." (Matthew 6:6).

Allow God's Word to speak to you right now. Silence your surroundings, be still, and meditate. Ask God to help you and use His Words to guide you.

7TH DAY: Take some time today to enjoy a Spirit-filled moment with the Lord and make a plan for developing new spiritual habits.

BENEDICTION: "The grace of the Lord Jesus Christ be with your spirit. Amen." (Philemon 1:25).

WEEK FOURTEEN: EL-SHADDAI – THE GOD WHO PROVIDES

Sovereign God, Mighty Savior,

You are the El-Shaddai, God Almighty, I make a joyful noise to let the world know that you are the most powerful God. After you, there is no other God. You are my Provider and Sustainer; nothing is lacking in my life because of You.

It is written in (Psalm 34:10): “The young lions suffer want and hunger; but those who seek the Lord lack no good thing.” I take you at your Word. Abraham was very old. You shepherded him. You had sent the Ravens to feed Elijah in the cave, so he did not go hungry.

When life is hard, when the pain is too much for me, even when there is a scarcity, you will provide for me and my family. Thank you in advance for seeing me through. This prayer is offered in the precious name of Jesus Christ, my Savior.
Amen.

Weekly Reflection

Are you a provider for your family, a friend, or your pets? Perhaps you are a provider in the sense that you regularly donate food items to your local food pantry or even a sponsor for a child living in another country.

Around Christians, we have numerous opportunities to help those in need as well as those close to us. How does God make use of you as a provider? Is there anyone in your congregation, workplace, or community who needs help this week? What are some simple but profound actions that you can take to help this person or others? Think about your relationship with God, your provider. The God who provides is never late or early. At the appointed time, He provides lavishly for His children.
God is capable of providing for our most pressing needs.
He will never abandon us to our own devices. We must always trust Him so that we do not have to worry about the things we fear we may lack. Remember that He sees you regardless of your difficulties, pain, or struggle.
Your problems, difficulties, and pain are not going unnoticed, and will never go unnoticed as long as you believe in His promises. God's provision may differ from what you expect, but He always provides. When was the last time you relied on God to provide for you? Reflect on that experience.

1ST DAY: BIBLE VERSE OF THE DAY: "The young lions suffer want and hunger. But those who seek the LORD lack no good thing." (Psalm 34:10).

What does this Bible verse show you about God?

2ND DAY: BIBLE VERSE OF THE DAY: "So we have to know and to believe the love that God has for us, God is love, and whoever abides in love and abides in God, and God abides in him." (John 4:16).

What is one thing you can do right now to get closer to God?

3RD DAY: BIBLE VERSE OF THE DAY: "And God is able to make all grace abound to you,so that having all sufficiency in all things at all times, you may abound in every good work." (2 Corinthians 9:8).

Think of a time when you prayed and God answered. Reflect on that time.

Write or say a prayer thanking God for how your prayers have been answered.

4TH DAY: BIBLE VERSE OF THE DAY: "Therefore you are great, O Lord God. For there is none like you, and there is no God besides you.

According to all that we have heard with our ears." (2 Samuel 7:22).

Write or say a prayer thanking God for His goodness.

5TH DAY: VERSE OF THE DAY: "I can do all things through him who strengthens me." (Philippians 4:13).

God is our source of strength. We must never forget that without Jesus, we are incomplete. Many of the things we do are only possible because of Him and only because of Him.

What are the three most recent things you were able to accomplish with God's help?

6TH DAY: BIBLE VERSE OF THE DAY: "The eyes of all look to you, and you give them their food in due season. You open your hand; you satisfy the desire of every living thing." (Psalm 145:15-16).

What did these verses teach me about God's character?

7TH DAY: Write or say a prayer of thanksgiving and praise.

BENEDICTION: "And the peace of God, which surpasses all understanding, will guard your hearts and your minds in Christ Jesus." (Philippians 4:7).

WEEK FIFTEEN: LIBERTY TO THE CAPTIVE

Mighty Warrior, the Lion of Judah, the Blessed Lamb of Calvary,

I approach your throne to cry before you for deliverance because I need a breakthrough, Lord. You performed miracles for the Israelites when they crossed the Red Sea on dry land. Moses struck the rock with your assistance, and water poured out for the people to drink. Lord, I beg you to break the bonds that bind me and set me free.

In the glorious name of Jesus, I rebuke every negative spirit.

Break every yoke of bondage. Lord, I entrust my life to You.

Lord, I also want to bring a woman in my community to you, who is suffering from confusion, abuse, drugs, or brainwashing. Please, give her clarity of purpose to surmount these challenges.

In the mighty name of Jesus, I pray that you break down all the barriers that keep her in bondage.

In the powerful name of Jesus, deliver her and destroy anything that binds her.

In the glorious name of Jesus, I rebuke every spirit of those who are never tired of tempting this woman. Please send your Archangel, Cherubim, and the Myriad Angels to protect her from all evil.

You came to free the prisoners and proclaim liberty to the captive.

Thank you for answering my prayer. I pray in the powerful name of Jesus.

Amen.

Weekly Reflection

The word "liberty" has different connotations for different people. My definition of liberty is the ability to do whatever you want within some boundaries. What does the word liberty mean to you?

The biblical concept of liberty differs from the world's concept of liberty. Christians' liberty needs structure. We are bound to Christ, who has liberated us to live according to His will. Christ has set us free. (Galatians 5:1) states, "For freedom Christ has set us free; stand firm therefore, and do not submit again to a yoke of slavery."

What are some of the things that are currently tying you up spiritually?
What are things that are preventing you from being free in Christ? Some people, for example, are bound by guilt. Others are bound by pride.

1ST DAY: BIBLE VERSE OF THE DAY: "So that we confidently say, 'The Lord is my helper, I will not be afraid. What will man do to me.'" (Hebrew 13:6).
What does this verse say about your value to God?

2ND DAY: BIBLE VERSE OF THE DAY: "Lord, how long will You look on? Rescue my soul from their ravages, My only life from the lions." (Psalm 35:17).

How do you feel after reading this verse?

3RD DAY: BIBLE VERSE OF THE DAY: "The Lord is a stronghold for the oppressed, a stronghold in times of trouble." (Psalm 9:9).

Meditate on this verse. Write or say a prayer thanking God for being there for you in your time of trouble.

4TH DAY: BIBLE VERSE OF THE DAY: "Vindicate me, O God, and plead my cause against an ungodly nation; O deliver me from the deceitful and unjust man!" (Psalm 43:1).

Write or pray to God for deliverance from any situation in which you are tempted to deny or disobey Him.

5TH DAY: BIBLE VERSE OF THE DAY: "Then they cried out to the Lord in their trouble; He saved them out of their distresses." (Psalm 107:19).

God always lifts up those who are down, helps those who have fallen, and provides for everyone. As believers of God, we can look to God to meet our needs. How can you use this Bible verse to encourage others?

6TH DAY: BIBLE VERSE OF THE DAY: "In your righteousness deliver me and rescue me; incline your ear to me, and save me!" (Psalm 71:2).

As Christians, you may be hated and persecuted at times.

Following Christ is not always easy, but it is always worthwhile.

Whatever life throws at you, the Lord is your refuge. When was the last time God used a difficult circumstance to help you grow in your faith?

7TH DAY: Take some time today to talk to your maker about what matters most in your life. Write or say a prayer thanking God for all of the blessings He has bestowed on you this week.

BENEDICTION: "And the peace of God, which surpasses all understanding, will guard your hearts and your minds in Christ Jesus." (Philippians 4:7).

WEEK SIXTEEN: A PRAYER FOR MARRIAGE RESTORATION

Glorious Lord and Heavenly Father,

I cannot cease praising you for your goodness and your mercy. Now, I want to thank you for this family that you put together. It is written in your Holy Word that two are better than one. I want to pray for this family who encountered some setbacks in their marriage.

Perform a miracle for them. I have read that you performed a great miracle at the wedding in Cana of Galilee. You turned water into wine. Please may you turn anger to love.

Restore this precious marriage and bind them together with a special code that won't be broken.

In the name of Jesus, I rebuke the spirit of division, the spirit of confusion, and lack of communication. Cover this family under the covenant of joy and love that never fails. I pray that every chain of anger, misunderstanding, and emotion be broken in the name of Jesus. I release your love without a limit for this family. In the mighty name of Jesus, I demolish the wall of division and anything that the enemy tries to use to divide and separate.

I convert the wall of bitterness into sweetness in the mighty name of Jesus. I rotate the lack of consideration into the ocean of love and the lack of patience into abundant grace.

I declare that today you send a load of kindness into this family house. In the glorious name of Jesus.

Amen.

Weekly Reflection

Marriage is a gift from God to enrich and fulfill our lives. God's plan for you and your husband is for you to live in peace and have a fun and meaningful relationship. The devil's strategy is for people to be at odds with one another. He is using every storm in the world against your marriage. You can defeat the devil by praying and pleading in Jesus's name. Remember, God is love, and after all, love is the most important thing, because it never fades, fails, or dies. Make time to pray in order to revitalize your marriage.

Many couples struggle to keep their marriages together. Others have a fulfilling marriage. Even in strong marriages, a few bumps in the road are to be expected. If you are married, what are some bumps that you are experiencing in your marriage? Have you brought it up to the Lord? What can you do to reap the benefits of a happy marriage? Do you recognize the importance of a spiritual, happy marriage and your role as a wife? If you are not married and hope to be one day, you can still respond by reflecting on your concept of a happy marriage as well as your role as a wife and a Christian woman. What can you do to make your marriage better? How do you prioritize God in your marriage? If you are not married, take the time to pray for a couple in your family, church, or community.

1ST DAY. BIBLE VERSE OF THE DAY: "Therefore, a man shall leave his father and his mother and hold fast to his wife, and they shall become one flesh." (Genesis 2:24).

Do you recall the first time you met your husband? Describe what happened that day and what drew your attention to your husband.

What are three characteristics of your husband that you admired early on in your relationship and continue to admire today? If you are not married yet, what are three characteristics that you hope your future husband might have?

Take a moment to say or write a prayer for your husband or future husband.

2ND DAY: BIBLE VERSE OF THE DAY: "Hear, O daughter, and consider, and incline your ear (to my instruction): forget your people and your father's house and the king will desire your beauty. Since he is your lord, bow to him. The people of Tyre will seek your favor with gifts, the richest of the people." (Psalm 45:10).

Write or say a prayer asking God to show you where you need to improve in your marriage.

3RD DAY: BIBLE VERSE OF THE DAY: "Unto him who can do immeasurably more tha all we ask or imagine, according to his power that is at work within us." (Ephesians 3:20).

Write or say a prayer asking God to help you love your husband and love each other more and grow closer to Him and to each other.

4TH DAY: BIBLE VERSE OF THE DAY: "In the same way, husbands should love their wives as their own bodies. He who loves his wife loves himself." (Ephesians 5:28).

What are your thoughts on this Bible verse?

5TH DAY: BIBLE VERSE FOR THE DAY: "Two are better than one, because they have a good return for their labor." (Ecclesiastes 4:9 NIV).

Write or say a prayer thanking God for your marriage if you have one. Or you could pray for the marriage of a loved one or a member of your congregation.

6TH DAY: BIBLE VERSE OF THE DAY: "Let marriage be held in honor among all, and let the marriage bed be undefiled, for God will judge the sexually immoral and adulterous. (Hebrews 13:4).

What is your interpretation of this Bible verse?

7TH DAY: If possible, set aside some time today to pray with your husband and children, if you have any. Invite God into your family, breaking the devil's yoke and releasing love and happiness in your home.

BENEDICTION: "The Lord bless you and keep you; the Lord make his face shine upon you and be gracious to you; The Lord lift up his countenance upon you and give you peace." (Numbers 6:24-26).

WEEK SEVENTEEN: A PRAYER FOR GUIDANCE AND PROTECTION FOR THE CHILDREN

Sovereign Lord, the Creature of the Universe,
Your Word in (Psalm 90:2) says, "Before the mountains were born you brought forth the whole world, from everlasting to everlasting you are God."

I come before you to thank you and pray for my children and grandchildren. Be with them as they confront whatever comes their way. Please, give me peace of mind as I entrust them to your capable hands.

Lord, I would also like to pray for the children in my family, church, and community. You created children and gave them opportunities to succeed in life.

Lord, I beseech you to keep all the children safe and away from harm.
I am concerned about various forms of negative social pressure, including abuse, bullying, and violence. Only You, O God, understand the challenges that children face on a daily basis.

Please, God, grant the children the capacity to differentiate between right and wrong. I know that you have a plan for every child. Lord, help them to be obedient and wise, as it is written in (Isaiah 1:19): "If you are willing and obedient, you will eat the good things of the land."

Jehovah Nissi, I am asking that you give all the parents inner peace when they are away from their children because it is not always easy.

I thank and praise you for all that you have done for my children, grandchildren,

children in my family, church, and community, and for all that you will continue to do in their lives. I pray in the precious name of Jesus Christ my Savior.

Amen.

There are numerous child protection policies in place in our society to ensure that children are not abused, mistreated, or hurt on a daily basis. This is not true in every part of the world.

Many abused children suffer not only physically but also emotionally and spiritually. We must protect children and provide them with love and security, as they are more vulnerable than adults. The future of your family, church, and community is dependent on the well-being of your children and all the children around you.

How would you describe your childhood? Did you grow up feeling safe and loved? How has your childhood experience affected your life today? If you had a rough abuse, have you ever prayed to God asking Him to heal you? Children are an integral part of God's grand plan for creation. We can't just stand there and watch the devil devour them like a lion. We must advocate for and provide for our children. Parents should teach their children about God because the absence of God in their lives is an open door for the enemy to enter.

"Let the little children come to me," Jesus said in (Isaiah 54:13). This invitation is sure proof that Jesus loves the children and always desires to be with them.

So, let us not be apprehensive about bringing our child(ren) to Jesus. Many children can find strength in having a solid foundation in Christ. This foundation, as well as their faith, can help them deal with life's challenges.

Support your child(ren), participate in their education, and be available to them. Bring them to church with you because their spiritual life is critical to their development.

What is your favorite thing to do with your child(ren)? What are some of the ways you help and advocate for your children? What do you want your child(ren) to remember the most about their childhood? For these questions, you can consider your grandchildren, nieces, nephews, or younger siblings. Write or say a prayer for your child(ren) or the children in your family, church, or community.

1ST DAY: BIBLE VERSE OF THE DAY: "Train up a child in the way he should go, even when he is old he will not depart from it." (Proverbs 22:6).

Parents are often their children's first educators, and it is their responsibility to teach their children life skills.

If you are a parent or have a child in your family, what are you doing as a Christian to properly educate your child(ren)?

2ND DAY: BIBLE VERSE OF THE DAY: "Can a woman forget her nursing child, that she should have no compassion on the son of her womb? Even these May forget you. Behold, yet I will not forget you. Behold, I have engraved you on the palms of my hands; your walls are continually before me." (Isaiah 49:15-16).

What can we learn about God from His written Word?

3RD DAY: BIBLE VERSE OF THE DAY: "A righteous man who walks in his integrity How blessed are his sons after him." (Proverbs 20:7).

You may believe that much is out of your hands.

You, on the other hand, have the ability to influence your children to follow God's path simply by living a righteous life.

This is significant because your children's future is determined by how you live your life on a daily basis.

How are you raising your child(ren) for God? What types of examples do you set for your children or the children around you?

4TH DAY: BIBLE VERSE OF THE DAY: "And the spirit of the Lord shall rest upon him, the spirit of wisdom and understanding, the spirit of counsel and might, the spirit of knowledge and of the fear of the Lord." (Isaiah 11:2).

Write or say a prayer to God, requesting wisdom and understanding

----

5TH DAY: BIBLE VERSE OF THE DAY: "And the child Samuel grew on, and was in favor both with the Lord and also with men." (1 Samuel 2:26).

Write or say a prayer for a child in your church or community.

6TH DAY: BIBLE VERSE OF THE DAY: "You shall teach them diligently to your children, and shall talk of them when you sit in your house, and when you walk by the way, and when you lie down, and when you rise." (Deuteronomy 6:7).

What does God reveal through His Word? Write or say a prayer for your child(ren) or the children in your family.

7TH DAY: Declare God's favor over your children in the precious name of Jesus.

BENEDICTION: "The Lord bless you and keep you; the Lord make his face shine on you and be gracious to you; the Lord turn his face toward you and give you peace." (Numbers 6:24-26).

WEEK EIGHTEEN: A PRAYER FOR PHYSICAL HEALING

Eternal Father,

The Healer of our bodies, I bow down before your throne to intercede for a touch from Your mighty hands. I know you are still in the business of healing your children. You have done it in the past. I strongly believe you will do it again.

You visited Peter's mother-in-law when she had a fever, and You immediately healed her. Please, move Heaven on Earth on behalf of my friend who desperately needs a miracle of healing today.

Please grant her the necessary strength, Lord.

I come to you asking that you may visit those who are afflicted with diseases such as high blood pressure, diabetes, backache, respiratory issues, breast cancer, Alzheimer's disease, heart disease, high cholesterol, and obesity. Help them be aware of your unfailing love and restore their health and heal their wounds, Lord.

I know Lord that your desire is for all your children to be in good physical and spiritual health to praise you.

As stated in (Isaiah 38:18 NIV), "For the grave cannot praise you, death cannot sing your praise; those who go down to the pit cannot hope for your faithfulness."

Thank you for answering my prayer. I ask for all these mercies in the powerful name of Jesus my Savior and my Lord.

Amen

Weekly Reflection

God created our bodies, and He expects us to care for them. God gave us our bodies as a gift to do His work. We are not able to do God's work when we are tired or if we are not able to think clearly. We are not able to glorify His name the way we should when we are physically unwell.

Our bodies are the temple of the living God. By taking care of our bodies and maintaining good health, we have the energy to serve God and minister to others.

By maintaining our health, we also can care for our loved ones and live a better life as well. Are there any major factors affecting your personal health, and overall wellness right now? What are you able to do this week to care for your physical body?

When was the last time you took the time to thank God for providing you with that most wonderful gift that is your body? Write or say a prayer thanking God for providing you with your physical body.

Many of us take good care of our physical health, but perhaps not our spiritual health. Are you aware that being spiritually healthy can help a person maintain their physical health? What do you do as God's child to maintain your spiritual health? Write down five simple ways you care for your spiritual health.

Write or say a prayer for someone in your family, church, or community to be healed. It is critical to pray for others.

1ST DAY: BIBLE VERSE OF THE DAY: "And God was doing extraordinary miracles by the hands of Paul." (Acts 19:11).

God has performed numerous extraordinary miracles. Consider your life and find an extraordinary miracle that God performed for you.

2ND DAY: VERSE OF THE DAY: "For I know the plans I have for you," declares the Lord, "plans to prosper you and not to harm you, plans to give you hope and a future." (Jeremiah 29:11).

What plans do you have for yourself this month? Do you think the plans you have this month match God's big plan for you? We can make plans, but God has the final say. Take a moment to bring your plans to God.

3RD DAY: BIBLE VERSE OF THE DAY: "Rejoice in hope, be patient in tribulation, be constant in prayer." (Romans 12:12).

When everything is going well, it is easy to rejoice. It may be difficult to be patient when faced with adversity. What aspect of your life requires patience?

Declare and make your request to God:

4TH DAY: BIBLE VERSE OF THE DAY: "For where two or three are gathered in my name, there am I among them." (Matthew 18-20).

Write or say a prayer for your church or any group of believers of Christ. It can be a prayer group.

5TH DAY: BIBLE VERSE OF THE DAY: "Jesus Christ is the same yesterday and today forever." (Hebrews 13:8).

What is your interpretation of this Bible verse?

6TH DAY: BIBLE VERSE OF THE DAY: "Bless the Lord, O my soul, and forget not all his benefits, who forgives all your iniquity, who heals all your -diseases." (Psalm 103:2-3).

What came to mind after reading these verses?

7TH DAY: Hallowed the name of the Lord for answering our prayer. Examine your week; is there anything you'd like to testify for God today?

BENEDICTION: "And the peace of God, which surpasses all understanding, will guard your hearts and your minds in Christ Jesus." (Philippians 4:7).

WEEK NINETEEN: A PRAYER FOR POWER TO FACE YOUR GIANTS WITH COURAGE

Dear Heavenly Father,

I glorify your name for your goodness and your mercy. I come before you with all the giants that want to persecute me. Every day I am confronted with giants that seek to destroy my life and peace of mind. I am confronted with problems, pressures, pain, persecutors, and diversions. I apply Jesus's blood and declare victory.

I arm myself with my spiritual armor in order to combat the giants who produce a grasshopper mentality in which I lose proper perspective.

Lord, some don't want good things for me. But since you are with me, there is nothing to worry about.

God, I beseech you to deliver those who are fighting their giant right now. I asked that you give them victory. I pray in the powerful name of Jesus, the captain of the Lord's army.

Amen.

Weekly Reflection

We all have had to face giants in our lives. What is a giant? Giants are not the product of a person's imagination, and they come in different forms. They try to rob us of inner peace and try to destroy our lives, relationships with our loved ones, and distract us from God's work. Giants are genuine issues, problems, or suffering.

The giant in your life might be financial issues, any form of abuse, under-employment, or unemployment. Your giant can be any form of addiction, depression, physical health issues, fear, anxiety, or phobia. What are the giants you are facing in your life today?

What can you do to conquer the everyday giants in your life?

Are you prepared spiritually to face your giants? Did you know that as a follower of Christ, you have the power of prayer to handle your giants? God is greater than your giants, and you can defeat them with the power of prayer. In (1 Thessalonians 5:16-18) states, "Rejoice always, pray without ceasing, give thanks in all circumstances; for this is the will of God in Christ Jesus for you."

Have you prayed to the Lord about your giants? Maybe you can pray to God about your Giants today. Write or say a prayer to God, requesting that He come and fight your battles.

1ST DAY: BIBLE VERSE OF THE DAY: "Be strong and courageous. Do not fear or be in dread of them, for it is the Lord your God who goes with you. He will not leave you or forsake you." (Deuteronomy 31:6).

God will never forsake you. Write or say a prayer of thanksgiving.

2ND DAY: BIBLE VERSE OF THE DAY: "For we do not wrestle against flesh and blood, but against the rulers, against the authorities, against the cosmic powers over this present darkness, against the spiritual forces of evil in the heavenly places." (Ephesians 6:12).

They are spiritual giants who operate at all hours of the day and night and are invisible to the naked eye. These giants cause conflicts and can be difficult to spot at times. As Christians, we must be prepared for any attack by donning God's armor. As Christians, we are equipped to fight spiritual warfare because we have the Word of God. Also, Christians are given prayer.

Describe the spiritual battle that exists in your life as a believer.

3RD DAY: BIBLE VERSE OF THE DAY: "Then they returned, every man of Judah and Jerusalem, and Jehoshaphat at their head, returning to Jerusalem with joy, for the Lord had made them rejoice over their enemies." (2 Chronicles 20:27).

Write or say a prayer of thanksgiving to God.

4TH DAY: BIBLE VERSE OF THE DAY: "Blessed be the Lord, my rock, who trains my hands for war, and my fingers for battle." (Psalm 144:1).

God had given you victory over your adversaries. Spend time rejoicing in God. How might you express your joy in God today? Write or say a prayer of praise to God.

5TH DAY: BIBLE VERSE OF THE DAY: "Who is the King of glory? The Lord is strong and mighty, the Lord is mighty in battle." (Psalm 24:8).

Take a moment to thank God for His many blessings.

6TH DAY: BIBLE VERSE OF THE DAY: "He trains my hands for battle so that my arms can bend a bow of bronze." (Psalm 18:34).

What does this verse convey to you after you've read it?

7TH DAY: Don't run away from your giants but run toward them. Your God is bigger than any giant.

How can you use what you learned this week in your life?

BENEDICTION: "And the peace of God, which surpasses all understanding, will guard your hearts and your minds in Christ Jesus." (Philippians 4:7).

WEEK TWENTY: A PRAYER AGAINST DOMESTIC VIOLENCE AND ABUSE

Dear God,

Thank you for this day. I come to you with some concerns, Lord.

You are aware of the number of children and adults in my community who have been victims of physical, mental, sexual, or other types of violence. Please God, visit them right now and liberate them.

Lord, grant the Spirit of discernment to those who believe that abuse is not real unless there is a physical bruise or to those who don't value themselves and think they deserve physical abuse and thus wait for bodily harm. Shine your light on them so they can see the truth.

God our Redeemer and Sustainer, we pray for the survivors of violence. Give your power to the powerless and heal their wounds, free them from fear, and restore them to true health. Lord, I pray for the healing of their families who have endured abuse and violence. You are the merciful Father and the God of comfort. Strengthen each person affected and help them face the future with faith.

I pray in the marvelous name of Jesus Christ, the King of kings and Lord of lords.

Amen.

Weekly Reflection

Abuse of any form is like a plague that can destroy you from the inside out. Have you experienced abuse in a relationship in any way, such as verbally, physically, emotionally, or financially, or have you been the victim of manipulation and domination? Perhaps you had a personal experience that left you feeling helpless, isolated, intimidated, or scared. The Bible says that if you find yourself in that type of situation, you must let go. (Hebrews 12:1-3) says, "Therefore, since we are surrounded by such a great cloud of witnesses, let us throw off everything that hinders and the sin that so easily entangles. And let us run with perseverance the race marked out for us, fixing our eyes on Jesus, the pioneer and perfecter of faith."

The message instructs you to throw away anything that impedes your progress or gets you easily entangled in sin.

What areas of your life do you need to let go of? What situation or specific thing in your life impedes or easily causes you entanglement?

Take a moment to pray and ask God what direction you should get rid of these things or situations.

1ST DAY: BIBLE VERSE OF THE DAY: "Be strong, and let your heart take courage, all you who wait for the Lord!" (Psalm 31:24).

As Christians, we are sometimes put under stress and pressure.

If we have faith in God and His timing, He will assist us in overcoming any obstacles that come our way. Write or say a prayer to God to help you trust Him and put your faith in Him.

2ND DAY: BIBLE VERSE OF THE DAY: "Let no corrupting talk come out of your mouths but only such as is good for building up, as fits the occasion, that it may give grace to those who hear." (Ephesians 4:29).

What does God reveal through His Word?

3RD DAY: BIBLE VERSE OF THE DAY: "Blessings are on the head of the righteous, but the mouth of the wicked conceals violence." (Proverbs 10:6).

Spend some time in prayer with God. Close your eyes, take a deep breath, visualize God on His throne, and declare that you are righteous.

4TH DAY: BIBLE VERSE OF THE DAY: "Love is patient and kind; love does not envy or boast; it is not arrogant or rude. It does not insist on its own way; it is not irritable or resentful; it does not rejoice at wrongdoing, but rejoices with the truth. Love bears all things, believes all things, hopes all things, endures all things." (1 Corinthians 13:4-7).

What significance do these Bible verses have in your life today?

5TH DAY: BIBLE VERSE OF THE DAY: "Who brought me out from my enemies; you exalted me above those who rose against me; you delivered me from men of violence." (2 Samuel 22:49).

According to the Bible, abuse or any form of violence is a sin in God's eyes. Write or say a prayer for the children or adults that are experiencing abuse or violence in your family, church, or community.

6TH DAY: BIBLE VERSE OF THE DAY: "And the peace of God, which surpasses all understanding, will guard your hearts and your minds in Christ Jesus." (Philippians 4:7)

God's peace is incomprehensible and unfathomable. To have "God's peace" is to put our faith in God even when we're afraid and anxious.

God is always there for us in the midst of our hardships. We must rely on our most potent weapon, prayer, to help us connect with Him.

Write or say a prayer asking God to grant us and our loved ones His peace.

7TH DAY: Fight for your loved ones and seize power to combat the forces of evil. Write or say a prayer thanking God for your loved ones.

BENEDICTION: "And the peace of God, which surpasses all understanding, will guard your hearts and your minds in Christ Jesus." (Philippians 4:7).

WEEK TWENTY-ONE: THE LORD WATCHES OVER ME AND MY FAMILY

Dear Heavenly Father,

My Lord and my good Shepherd, I come before you to adore and glorify your holy name that is above all names. I lift up my eyes to you now seeking help. I know my help will come from You.

Today, I pray that you will deliver me and my family members from our brokenness, helplessness, despair, and hopelessness.

Yahweh, sometimes, I feel shattered, as if I'm walking through the valley of the shadow of death, unable to find my way out. But I'm not afraid because you're with me.

You are my keeper, Holy Father, so thank you for carefully watching over me and my family and ensuring that we are well protected.

Lord, I am favored and secure beneath your wings. I am protected by your shadow, Lord.

When I see how much evil goes unpunished in this world, it makes me sad at times. I read, see, and hear about women and girls who are abused, kidnapped, and treated as trash.

The beautiful world you created has become strange and full of hatred, envy, and greed for money. Throughout it all, you promise to keep your children safe from harm, but danger remains. So I know help is on the way.

Lord, I thank you for everything you've done for me and my family, as well as everything you'll do for us in the future. I pray in the mighty name of Jesus. Amen.

Weekly Reflection

We all need someone to keep an eye on us because life can be frightening at times. We all need someone who is concerned about us. A person who can simply lend a shoulder to lean and cry on when we are in trouble. As Christians, we have a God who watches over us. What a relief to know that our Savior is watching over us! We must speak God's promise over ourselves and our loved ones because claiming the Lord's promise directly tells Him that we trust Him to keep an eye on us and our loved ones. We can live confidently as God's children without being paralyzed by fear, disaster, or false beliefs. "The eyes of the Lord are toward the righteous and his ears toward their cry" (Psalm 34:15). Every promise of God's protection is meant for you and me and as a result, we have many testimonies of where God protected us. Reflect and describe a situation in which you felt that if it hadn't been for God's protection, you would not be here today.

When was the last time you talked to God about your safety? Do you take the time to thank God for keeping you and your family safe on a daily basis?

Write or say a prayer for the safety of yourself and your family.

Also, thank Him for protecting you daily.

1ST DAY: BIBLE VERSE OF THE DAY: "I am with you and will watch over you wherever you go,

and I will bring you back to this land. I will not leave you until I have done what I have promised you." (Genesis 28:15).

God promises to be with you every step of the way, and He has a plan for your future. What meaning does God's promise have for you? Does His promise provide you with confidence as you live your daily life?

2ND DAY: BIBLE VERSE OF THE DAY: "A land that the Lord your God cares for.

The eyes of the Lord your God are always upon it, from the beginning of the year to the end of the year." (Deuteronomy 11:12).

Close your eyes and breathe the name of the Lord in prayer. Take the time to express appreciation for His promises.

3RD DAY: BIBLE VERSE OF THE DAY: "The LORD will keep you from all harm. He will watch over your life; the LORD will watch over your coming and going, both now and forevermore." (Psalm 121:7-8).

God is always watching over you. This may not always appear to you to be the case.

If things don't go as planned, you may believe God has abandoned you.

This is never the case because He is always with you.

Have you ever felt as if God had abandoned you? If you've never felt that way, you might at some point in your life.

What can you do in this situation or with this emotion? If you ever feel this way, don't dwell on these feelings. Take the time to pray and read all His promises from the Bible where He promises to watch over you. You can completely trust His Words.

Spend some time with God, thanking Him for His Words, and assurances.

4TH DAY: BIBLE VERSE OF THE DAY: "The LORD is your keeper; the LORD is your shade on your right hand." (Psalm 121:5).

Do you believe that God will always protect you? How has God protected you thus far this year?

5TH DAY: BIBLE VERSE OF THE DAY: "I will instruct you and teach you in the way you should go; I will counsel you with my eye upon you." (Psalm 32:8).

Have you ever felt that God was teaching you through an experience? Do you find it difficult to learn about learning lessons from God? What are some strategies for increasing your understanding of God's Words or learning about God through experience?

6TH DAY: BIBLE VERSE OF THE DAY: "Have I not commanded you? Be strong and courageous. Do not be frightened, and do not be dismayed, for the Lord your God is with you wherever you go." (Joshua 1:9).

What did you learn about God from this Bible verse?

7TH DAY: Today, Father, I choose to direct my struggle and fear toward you, the All-Knowing and All-Powerful. In the name of mighty God, I pray. Amen.

BENEDICTION: "And the peace of God, which surpasses all understanding, will guard your hearts and your minds in Christ Jesus." (Philippians 4:7).

WEEK TWENTY-TWO: A PRAYER FOR BREAKING THE GENERATIONAL CURSE

Dear God, Heavenly Father,

I praise you because of who you are and all that you have done for me. I thank you for that wonderful statement of victory.
Lord, you have redeemed me and I am free from the generational curses.
Thank you for your blood on Calvary's cross that destroyed the power of the enemies.
Oh glory to you mighty God, you have ransomed me and my family.
Today Father, I declare that you are the only Savior, the Lion of Judah, and the Lamb that was slain for me. Oh, I am thankful!

Today, Heavenly Father, I claim your blood that flowed over the roots of all the curses against me and my family members to be uprooted, destroyed, and died out in the mighty name of Jesus.

In the mighty name of Jesus Christ, I declare war on every generational curse and its manifestations of sickness, and bad habits from parents or grandparents such as alcohol, addiction, smoking addiction, drug addiction, financial problems, spiritual oppression, obsession, premature death, destruction, emotional instability, anger, abuse, and depression.

Thank you for giving your children the ability to destroy the power of their adversaries, so I take up my weapon against fear, enslaving habits, drugs, immoral sex, eating disorders, obesity, irrational behavior, spiritual blindness, confusion, depression, bad decisions, idol worship, ongoing family conflicts, mental illness, procrastination, rebellion, feelings of inadequacy, growing marital issues, serial cheating, and restlessness. I know you can break these curses, and in Jesus's name, I command the Holy Spirit to destroy all satanic plantings and strongholds.

Your Word in (Romans 8:1) teaches me that "There is now no condemnation for those who are in Christ Jesus." By your power, I am persuaded that the negative habits of my grandparents or parents won't transfer to me because I am free indeed. Thank you for victory. I pray in the mighty name of Jesus Christ.
Amen.

Weekly Reflection

What is a generational curse? I define a generational curse as something that is passed down from one generation to the next. It can be a bad habit. It can be a negative way of life, behavior, or preferences. It is destructive, as evidenced by alcoholism, domestic abuse, drug abuse, or some parents' inability to be affectionate. How can one be certain of the existence of this curse? A generational curse may exist if you observe a pattern of negative behavior among family members of different generations.

Reflect on your family, especially your parents, grandparents, aunts, and uncles, for any sinful habits, preferences, lifestyle, or conduct. Is it possible for you to identify any generational curses in your family? How about in your own life? Have you noticed any patterns or recurring issues that you believe have passed from a previous generation?

As a child of Christ, what can you do about the possibility of a generational curse in your family? God's Word clearly stated, "There is therefore now no condemnation for those who are in Christ Jesus." (Romans 8:1). God also says in (Hebrew 8:12), "For I will be merciful toward their iniquities, and I will remember their sins no more." Christ is the antidote to all generational curses. Christ is your remedy for escaping a generational curse. As Christians, we can have a fresh start in Christ, and God will no longer remember our sins. We will have eternal life if we trust in Him. Write or say a prayer to God thanking Him for eternal life. Take a moment to bring any and all generational curses to Him in prayer

----

1ST DAY: BIBLE VERSE OF THE DAY: "For we do not wrestle against flesh and blood, but against the rulers, against the authorities, against the cosmic powers over this present darkness, against the spiritual forces of evil in the heavenly places." (Ephesians 6:12).

How do you interpret this biblical verse?

2ND DAY: BIBLE VERSE OF THE DAY: "You shall not bow down to them or serve them, for I the Lord your God am a jealous God, visiting the iniquity of the fathers on the children to the third and for the generation of those who hate me." (Exodus 29:5).

What can you do as a Christian to break bad cycles or habits that have plagued your family? What measures can be taken to prevent its transmission to the next generation? If you have children or grandchildren, what can you do to prevent them from picking up undesirable behaviors from previous generations?

3RD DAY: BIBLE VERSE OF THE DAY: "Christ redeemed us from the curse of the law by becoming a curse for us, for it is written, 'Cursed is everyone who is hanged on a tree.'" (Galatians 3:13).

Christ paid the price for you when He died on the cross. God demonstrates His own love for us in this act. How has Christ redeemed you?

4TH DAY: BIBLE VERSE OF THE DAY: "Therefore, there is now no condemnation for those who are in Christ Jesus, because through Christ Jesus the law of the Spirit who gives life has set you free from the law of sin and death." (Romans 8:1-2).

Write or say a prayer of thanksgiving:

5TH DAY: BIBLE VERSE OF THE DAY: "Submit yourselves, then, to God. Resist the devil, and he will flee from you." (James 4:7).

Do you believe that God will always provide you with everything you require? God a dores you. He knows everything about you. He is interested in your life and wants to be a part of it.

As a Christian, He instructs you to resist the devil and place your complete trust in Him. Take a few moments to write or say a prayer to God asking for the strength you need to resist the devil.

6TH DAY: BIBLE VERSE OF THE DAY: "And the peace of God, which surpasses all understanding, will guard your hearts and your minds in Christ Jesus." (Philippians 4:7). As Christians, we receive peace from God which is the peace of the Holy Spirit. This peace is different from the peace that the world offers.

How can we ensure the peace of God in our lives? It is accomplished through prayer regardless of the situation. Take a moment to write or say a prayer of gratitude.

7TH DAY: Take a moment to pray for a family member who is struggling with a bad habit or negative behavior, or who is simply trying to get out of a bad situation.

BENEDICTION: "And the peace of God, which surpasses all understanding, will guard your hearts and your minds in Christ Jesus." (Philippians 4:7).

WEEK TWENTY-THREE: A PRAYER OF PRAISE AND ADORATION

I adore and worship you, Father because you are worthy of all praise.

In (Psalm 34:3), David invited everyone to come and worship Him, saying, "Come, let us tell of the Lord's greatness; let us exalt his name together."

Lord, I see your handy work when I look around the universe.

The deep blue ocean, sea creatures of all kinds, the waves, and the strong breeze all speak of your most powerful and supernatural ability.

When I see all of the different trees, plants, and birds in the fields, I think to myself, "How wonderful You are."

There is no other power that can do these things.

Every day, I watch the sun rise in the morning and set in the evening.

I say like David in (Psalm 8:1): "O Lord, our Lord, how majestic is your name in all the earth! You have set your glory above the heavens."

"Hallowed be your Name!" I come before you with awe in my heart and acknowledge your greatness, as David prayed in (1 Chronicles 29:11): "Yours, O Lord, is the greatness and the power and the glory and the victory and the majesty, for all that is in the heavens and in the earth is yours. Yours is the kingdom, O Lord, and you are exalted as head above all."

I ask all these mercies in the mighty name of Jesus, the King of kings and Lord of lords.

How majestic is your name in all the earth! Hallowed be your Name today and forever.

Amen.

Have you met anyone who has made a difference in your life? Have you taken the time to express your heartfelt appreciation to this person?

Perhaps you had a supervisor who was an excellent leader and mentor.

In this case, you took the time to thank the individual for being an exceptional leader.

Maybe it was your teacher, and you thanked the teacher for instilling in you the confidence to pursue lofty goals or for providing you with the necessary academic skills for success.

What about the all-powerful God, the creator of the universe and the ruler of the world, the source of salvation, and the Holy One who gives you everything you have?

How much more does He deserve your love and admiration?

Have you given Him thanks for His extraordinary greatness, holiness, mercy and compassion, and faithfulness?

Write about some ways you have expressed your gratitude to God.

God has been so gracious to you, and you should always sing His praises.

In (Psalm 156:6), David wrote, "Let everything that has breath praise the Lord. Praise the Lord." It's incredible what praising can do for you. As a Christian, how do you express your praise to God? What words can you use to praise Him for what you have and all He has done for you? For this week, I challenge you to spend an extra five minutes per day praising and worshiping God. Not only should you thank Him, but you should also praise Him. Allow the Holy Spirit to accept your offering of adoration and praise. Write or say a prayer of praise to God for His love and kindness.

1ST DAY: BIBLE VERSE OF THE DAY: "Lord, you are my God; I will exalt you; I will praise your name for you have done wonderful things, plans formed of old, faithful, and sure." (Isaiah 25:1).

Today, I praise God for:

What can you do for God today to express your praise?

2ND DAY: BIBLE VERSE OF THE DAY: "Let everything that has breath praise the Lord! Praise the Lord!" (Psalm 150:6).

Today, I praise God for:

What can you do for God today to express your praise?

3RD DAY: BIBLE VERSE OF THE DAY: "Bless the Lord, O my soul, and all that is within me, bless his holy name!" (Psalm 103:1).

Today, I praise God for:

What can you do for God today to express your praise?

4TH DAY: BIBLE VERSE OF THE DAY: "I will give thanks to the Lord with my whole heart; I will recount all of your wonderful deeds." (Psalm 9:1).

Today, I praise God for:

What can you do for God today to express your praise?

5TH DAY: BIBLE VERSE OF THE DAY: "Great is the Lord, and greatly to be praised and his greatness is unsearchable." (Psalm 145:3).

Today, I praise God for:

What can you do for God today to express your praise?

6TH DAY: BIBLE VERSE OF THE DAY: "My mouth is filled with your praise, and with your glory all the day." (Psalm 71:8).

Today, I praise God for:

What can you do for God today to express your praise?

7TH DAY: Lift your hands and praise God for His continued blessings. Write or say a prayer of praise to God.

BENEDICTION: "The Lord bless you and keep you; the Lord make his face shine upon you and be gracious to you; the Lord lift up his countenance upon you and give you peace. 'So shall they put my name upon the people of Israel, and I will bless them.'" (Numbers 6:24-27).

WEEK TWENTY-FOUR: A PRAYER FOR SINGLE MOTHERS

Most Merciful God,

All-Knowing, I worship and adore you for your greatness. Your knowledge is unlimited.

Lord, I come to you today to pray for a single mom in my church. You are familiar with her and her situation. She is currently having a tough time working and raising her children. Lord, you know all of her struggles.

Everything appears to be falling on her shoulders. Lord, she needs your help to survive. Heavenly Father, you will do much more for them. Shepherd them, Lord.

Provide for her family in the name of Jesus, just as you did for Abraham with the lamb for the burnt offering.

Amen.

Weekly Reflection

It can be tough for some single mothers, as they have to raise children, manage their homes, keep a budget, and live life in general. If you are a single mother, the good news is that God won't forget you. As a single mother, it is important to build a support system, find a way to manage your finances, pray for wisdom and direction, and believe in God's promises.

(James 1:6 NIV) says, "But when you ask, you must believe and not doubt, because the one who doubts is like a wave of the sea, blown and tossed by the wind." If you are a single mother, what is your biggest struggle? If you are not a single mother, how can you support a single mother in your family, church, or community?

Write a prayer for a single mother that you know who might be in a difficult situation. God who sees and cares loves you. If you are a single mother, write or say a prayer for your life and family life.

1ST DAY: BIBLE VERSE OF THE DAY: "Say to those who have an anxious heart, "Be strong; fear not! Behold, your God will come with vengeance, with the recompense of God. He will come and save you." (Isaiah 35:4).

God is with you and will be with you and guide you no matter what you are going through.

2ND DAY: BIBLE VERSE OF THE DAY: "The angel of the LORD also said to her, "I will surely multiply your offspring so that they cannot be numbered for multitude." (Genesis 16:10).

Hagar was the first single parent identified in the Bible. How did God help her in her difficult moment?

3RD DAY: BIBLE VERSE OF THE DAY: "Call to me and I will answer you, and will tell you great and hidden things that you have not known." (Jeremiah 33:3).

Take the time to write or say a prayer to God, and God will reveal great things to you.

4TH DAY: BIBLE VERSE OF THE DAY: "So she called the name of the LORD who spoke to her, 'You are a God of seeing,' for she said, 'Truly here I have seen him who looks after me.'" (Genesis 16:13).

You belong to God. God sees you and will be there for you in every situation and ensure that you are protected and guided in the right direction.

5TH DAY: BIBLE VERSE OF THE DAY: "You Father of the fatherless and protector of widows is God in his holy habitation." (Psalm 68:5).

After reading this Bible verse, what are some of the thoughts running through your mind?

6TH DAY: BIBLE VERSE OF THE DAY: "Do your best to present yourself to God as one approved, a worker who has no need to be ashamed, rightly handling the word of truth." (2 Timothy 2:15).

What does this Bible verse reveal to you?

7TH DAY: Reflect on what you have learned about what God has done for Hagar.

BENEDICTION: "And the peace of God, which surpasses all understanding, will guard your hearts and your minds in Christ Jesus." (Philippians 4:7).

WEEK TWENTY-FIVE: A PRAYER TO FIGHT CHRONIC FATIGUE

Dear God, the Lion of of Judah, I come before your throne of grace to find favor for this woman who suffers from chronic fatigue. I claim power and authority over this fatigue that your servant has to continuously deal with.

Dear Lord, you know how she feels. She is worn out and overwhelmed. It is very difficult for her to function well in this society and live a healthy life. Lord, she feels exhausted and needs your strength. Please break this chain of fatigue and refresh her spirit. She is exhausted and needs Your strength. Please, fill her emptiness, restore her mind, and energize her heart so that she will function properly and live a better life. In the mighty name of Jesus, I declare this strange fatigue to be away from her mind and body, away from her life, and never to return in the mighty name of Jesus.

Please, put your blood on the door of her house so that the enemy will stay away; give her the courage to rebuke whatever may drain her rather than feed her. Please, give her the power to overcome. I pray in the precious name of Jesus. Amen.

Weekly Reflection

What is chronic fatigue? I define chronic fatigue as having insufficient energy to function properly day to day.

It is a common complaint heard frequently in modern life and is caused by a number of different circumstances.

However, spiritual fatigue is characterized as feeling exhausted, depleted, disheartened, or despondent in one's Christian walk. Many Christians experience spiritual fatigue at some point in their lives.

Have you experienced spiritual fatigue?

When was the last time you experienced spiritual fatigue?

How have you dealt with spiritual fatigue? What are some signs of spiritual fatigue?

How did you overcome spiritual fatigue in the past?

Is it your first instinct to express your feelings to God when you are feeling exhausted, depleted, or disheartened in your spiritual walk with God?

Write or say a prayer, asking God for the strength to carry and propel you onward.

Ask God to help you gain the Holy Spirit's power that you need.

1ST DAY: BIBLE VERSE OF THE DAY: "I can do all things through him who strengthens me." (Philippians 4:13).

What does God's Word impart to you?

2ND DAY: BIBLE VERSE OF THE DAY: "Do not be anxious about anything, but in every situation, by prayer and petition, with thanksgiving, present your requests to God. And the peace of God, which transcends all understanding, will guard your hearts and your minds in Christ Jesus." (Philippians 4:6-7 NIV).

What does the Bible say about feeling fatigued?

3RD DAY: BIBLE VERSE OF THE DAY: "Submit yourselves therefore to God. Resist the devil, and he will flee from you." (James 4:7).

What steps can you take today to submit yourself to God?

4TH DAY: BIBLE VERSE OF THE DAY: "All Scripture is breathed out by God and profitable for teaching, for reproof, for correction, and for training in righteousness." (2 Timothy 3:16).

What does this Bible verse reveal to you?

5TH DAY: BIBLE VERSE OF THE DAY: "Come to me, all who labor and are heavy laden, and I will give you rest. Take my yoke upon you, and learn from me, for I am gentle and lowly in heart, and you will find rest for your souls. For my yoke is easy, and my burden is light." (Matthew 11 28-30).

Take the time to bring your burden to God. When life's concerns weigh us down, we do not have to carry the heavy load on our own! God is willing to carry our burden. Write or say a prayer to God bringing our burdens to Him.

6TH DAY: BIBLE VERSE OF THE DAY: "He gives power to the faint, and to him who has no might he increases strength." (Isaiah 40:29).

We need spiritual strength to persevere faithfully. Take a moment, find a quiet location, and express your feelings to God.

7TH DAY: Speak the word of energy on your body in the name of Jesus. Declare it now.

BENEDICTION: "Say to them: 'The Lord bless you and keep you; the Lord make his face shine upon you and be gracious to you; the Lord lift up his countenance upon you and give you peace.' So shall they put my name upon the people of Israel, and I will bless them." (Numbers 6:24-27).

WEEK TWENTY-SIX: MY STRUGGLES ARE NOT FINAL

The Mighty Warrior, the Lion of the tribe of Judah, today is the day that you have made and I am delighted that my difficulties are temporary with you. I know when you are at the vessel, I can laugh at the storm because it is your last word that matters. (Romans 8:31) states that "If you are for us, who can be against us?" Therefore, I refuse to live in captivity. Lord, I pray that you will replace my distress with peace, and that you will be my strength when I am weak and unable to continue.

I come to you, Lord, to bring a couple of people to prayer.
I refuse to accept that my loved one will live in poverty.
I know her health will be restored because her illness is only temporary.
I am confident she will have peace in her home.
Lord, I believe that the young woman, you know her name and nature will be promoted at work, her finances will improve, her children will succeed, and her status will change. She will rejoice in Your name, Lord, because her financial situation is only temporary.

Today, I want to roll up my sleeves and fight for victory. In the Mighty name of Jesus, I declare that I am strong, and victorious, and that I will succeed in my endeavors. I am in good health, Lord. I will shine, and I will have enough money to care for myself and my family. In the wonderful name of Jesus, I pray. Amen.

Weekly Reflection

What are your dreams in life? Take some time to reflect on your dreams. Do you believe you're living the dream? Have you ever taken the time to express your dreams to God? Have you checked to see if your dreams line up with God's plans? God has grand plans for our lives. God wants us to have dreams. He wants you to pursue your dreams when they align with your true desires, His Word, and His Will. He gave us ambitions and aspirations so that we could achieve greater things in Christ. Reflect on your hopes and dreams for the future. Are they aligned with your true desires, His Word, and His Will?

1ST DAY: BIBLE VERSE OF THE DAY: "And after you have suffered a little while, the God of all grace, who has called you to his eternal glory in Christ, will himself restore, confirm, strengthen and establish you." (1 Peter 5:10).

In this life, we will face physical, societal, or moral obstacles and suffering will occur, but it will cease for those who have faith in Christ. How do you deal with obstacles in life that impede you from reaching your objectives and living your dream?

Did you pray to God during times of suffering?

Don't give up. Peter never did. Reflect on your experiences.

2ND DAY: BIBLE VERSE OF THE DAY: "For the LORD your God is he who goes with you to fight for you against your enemies, to give you the victory." (Deuteronomy 20:4).

Write or say a prayer for wisdom on how to approach your difficulties.

3RD DAY: BIBLE VERSE OF THE DAY: "Count it all joy, my brother, when you meet trials of various kinds, for you know that the testing of your faith produces steadfastness. And let steadfastness lacking in nothing." (James 1:2-4).

What does James mean by "count it all joy"?

What changes should I make to my life in light of the message contained in these verses?

4TH DAY: BIBLE VERSE OF THE DAY: "There is therefore now no condemnation for those who are in Christ Jesus." (Romans 8:1).

What does the Bible say it means to be in Christ Jesus?

5TH DAY: BIBLE VERSE OF THE DAY: "God is our refuge and strength, a very present help in trouble." (Psalm 46:1). Take a few minutes to meditate on God's Words.

6TH DAY: BIBLE VERSE OF THE DAY: "For we know him who said, 'Vengeance is mine: I will replay.' And again, The Lord will judge his people." (Hebrew 10:30).

What does this Bible verse reveal to you?

7TH DAY: Take a moment to pray for victory over any stronghold.

Before starting, inhale deeply, then gently exhale. Let go of those things that are not of God. Now, invite God into your moment of prayer.

BENEDICTION: "The Lord bless you and keep you; the Lord make his face shine upon you and be gracious to you; the Lord lift up his countenance upon you and give you peace. 'So shall they put my name upon the people of Israel, and I will bless them.'" (Numbers 6:24-27).

WEEK TWENTY-SEVEN: A PRAYER FOR IDENTITY CRISIS

O Lord Almighty, I bless your holy name, worship You in humble adoration. I bring my burden to you, the burden of an identity crisis. My identity dilemma weighs heavily on me, but I am confident that you will act on my side.

Lord, assist me in recognizing when I place my identity in something other than you. You have done it for Jabez, who had the same challenge. He refused to remain the way he was born. He renounced the awful meaning of his name. You, O Lord, changed his status. Instead of pain, sadness, and misery, You changed it to a celebration. He became the most honorable.

I know, you can change my status from pain to honorable as you have done for Jabez. Yes, Lord, you converted Hanna's barrenness to fertility, Ruth's widowhood to marriage, Esther's orphanhood to queenhood, and Mary Magdalene's demonic possession to discipleship.

I refuse to allow others to determine my identity. I don't want to keep up with others on social media or in my immediate vicinity, but today I resolve not to let anyone or anything press me down for what I am not or don't have.

In the name of Jesus, thank you for seeing me through and granting me my heart's desire.

Amen.

Weekly Reflection

Many of us are very interested in discovering our own identity. As a result, Ancestry DNA kits, and family trees are all quite popular nowadays. People are eager to learn more about their physical identity and heritage. They want to discover their ancestors. It is amazing what we can learn about ourselves and our roots. We have others that are experiencing an identity crisis that may be rooted in their sentiments and wellness, and they are seeking treatment to cope with periods of uncertainty in their lives.

Many have periodically faced a time in their lives when they felt uncertain about their identity. What about you? Have you ever experienced an identity crisis? A period where you had trouble figuring out who you were and your sense of self was insecure or less stable. Maybe you are experiencing that right now in your life, and you seem unsure of who you are, and you might be questioning or doubting yourself or your purpose.

However, the Bible teaches that we are all created in God's image. (Genesis 1:26-27) states the following: "Then God said, 'Let us make man in our image, after our likeness. And let them have dominion over the fish of the sea and over the birds of the heavens and over the livestock and over all the earth and over every creeping thing that creeps on the earth.' So God created man in his own image, in the image of God he created him; male and female he created them."

Our core Christian identity is built and grounded in Him. When we lose sight of the plan that our Creator planned for us, we experience an identity crisis. As a result, God desires that we read His Word in order to discover our true identity. Take a moment and open your Bible to read (Ephesians 2:19) and (2 Corinthians 9:8). God bestows the ability to recognize oneself.

It is critical that you continue your education, pursue your career, improve your business, and get a good job if that is the desire of your heart and part of God's plan. But your identity in Jesus Christ is the most important of all these things. What factors can contribute to an identity crisis in your life? Take some time to analyze what might be triggering an identity crisis in your life if you are experiencing one. If it was anything in the past, consider what you believed caused your identity issue. Have you experienced an identity crisis before? If so, did you ever pray to God about an identity crisis you had in the past? Do you believe this experience helped you improve spiritually? What have you taken away from this experience? Do you have a trusted friend who is a Christian whom you may approach to pray for you if you are going through an identity crisis? It might be really good to invite others to pray for you and remind you of the truth. A Christian who is further along in their faith journey than you can provide valuable insight as you walk with Jesus. Consider asking a fellow Christian to assist you in areas where you are having difficulty.

1ST DAY: BIBLE VERSE OF THE DAY: "So then you are no longer strangers and aliens, but you are fellow citizens with the saints and members of the household of God." (Ephesians 2:19).

You are not a stranger; you are a member of God's family. Take some time to consider your identity in Christ and answer the question, "Who does God call you to be?"

2ND DAY: BIBLE VERSE OF THE DAY: "And we know that for those who love God all things work together for good, for those who are called according to his purpose." (Romans 8:28).

Write or utter a prayer to God, requesting that He overthrow all plans that are opposed to His plan for your life.

3RD DAY: BIBLE VERSE OF THE DAY: "So God created man in his own image, in the image of God he created him; male and female he created them." (Genesis 1:27).

Reflect on God's Words:

4TH DAY: BIBLE VERSE OF THE DAY: "But you are a chosen race, a royal priesthood, a holy nation, a people for his own possession, that you may proclaim the excellencies of him who called you out of darkness into his marvelous light." (1 Peter 2:9).

How does this verse generate your delight in Christ?

5TH DAY: BIBLE VERSE OF THE DAY: "Before I formed you in the womb I knew you, and before you were born, I consecrated you; I appointed you a prophet to the nations." (Jeremiah 1:5).

Reflect on God's Words.

6TH DAY: BIBLE VERSE OF THE DAY: "For in Christ Jesus, you are all sons of God, through faith." (Galatians 3:26).

Are there any changes you should make in your life based on what God revealed to you in this verse?

7TH DAY: Pray for the strength to live the life God intended for you to live.

BENEDICTION: "And the peace of God, which surpasses all understanding, will guard your hearts and your minds in Christ Jesus." (Philippians 4:7).

WEEK TWENTY-EIGHT: A PRAYER FOR FORGIVENESS OF SINS

Gracious Lord, the Forgiver of sin, I bow down before you begging for forgiveness for all my iniquities. Please God, have pity on me according to your unfailing love and your great compassion.

I asked that you forgive me for the hurtful words I have spoken. I deeply regret anything I've done wrong.
I beseech you to help me to forgive my offender and all those who harmed me.
I know You are faithful and just to forgive our sins and cleanse us from all unrighteousness.

I take you at your word today and ask for a complete wash away of all my guilt.
I know when you forgive, you forget and remember them no more.

In the magnificent name of Jesus, I ask you to cleanse my heart and fill my mind with love and kindness.
Amen.

Weekly Reflection

What exactly does the term "forgiveness" mean? I describe forgiveness as no longer being angry or letting the person off the hook for the person who did wrong. It is also said that forgiveness is a decision we make based on our willingness to obey God and His command to forgive.

God wants you to be kind to others and let go of any grudges you might have against another person. (Colossians 3:13 NIV) states: "Bear with each other and forgive one another if any of you has a grievance against someone.
Forgive as the Lord forgave you." Why is forgiveness so important? What do you think is the advantage of forgiving others?

Sometimes, we claimed to have forgiven a person. We forgave the person from the mouth but not from the heart? Have you just forgiven a person from your mouth and not from your heart? How would you know if you truly forgive a person who has wronged you?

1ST DAY: BIBLE VERSE OF THE DAY: "Whoever conceals his transgressions will not prosper, but he who confesses and forsakes them will obtain mercy." (Proverbs 28:13).

What adjustments should I make in my life as a result of this verse?

2ND DAY: BIBLE VERSE OF THE DAY: "For you, O Lord, are good and forgiving, abounding in steadfast love to all call upon you." (Psalm 86:5).

What does this Bible verse reveal about God's glory?

3RD DAY: BIBLE VERSE OF THE DAY: "Then Peter came up and said to him, 'Lord, how often will my brother sin against me, and I forgive him? As many as seven times?' Jesus said to him, 'I do not say to you seven times, seven-seven times.'"

(Matthew 18:21-22).

What do these verses teach you about God, and about yourself?

4TH DAY: BIBLE VERSE OF THE DAY: "For I will forgive their wickedness and will remember their sins no more." (Hebrew 8:12).

Write or say a prayer for someone who has wronged you and whom you have either forgiven or are struggling to forgive.

5TH DAY: BIBLE VERSE OF THE DAY: "Walk in wisdom toward outsiders, making the best use of the time. Let your speech always be gracious, seasoned with salt, so that you may know how you ought to answer each person." (Colossians 4:5-6).

What does the Word of God reveal to you?

6TH DAY: BIBLE VERSE OF THE DAY: "If we confess our sins, he is faithful and just to forgive us our sins and to cleanse us from all unrighteousness." (1 John 1:9).

God promises those who confess their sins that they will be forgiven. Is there anything you should confess to God? Take a moment to reflect and then confess to God.

7TH DAY: Make a list of the miracles you believe God will do for you.

BENEDICTION: "And the peace of God, which surpasses all understanding, will guard your hearts and your minds in Christ Jesus." (Philippians 4:7).

WEEK TWENTY-NINE: A PRAYER FOR HEALING

Heavenly Father, the Great Healer. You are Jehovah Rapha. At this moment, I humbly bow before you to praise you for your marvelous deed. Thank you for your love and your kindness.

You say in your Words, "Ask, and it will be given to you," so I come to beg you to heal my body. Yes, Father, you made heaven and earth, and the world belongs to you. When we pray for the different storms in our lives to be stilled, doors are made open, and sick people get healing as a result.

Today, I pray for all those who are ill or in pain. Please, Yahweh, heal your servants and help them overcome their sickness and anguish in Jesus's name.

I declare and decree that asthma is no longer a part of the life of my loved one.

I declare and decree that fibroid is out in the life of my loved one in the name of Jesus.

I declare and decree that pain in the chest, chronic inflammation, and prostate cancer be cast out from the lives of my loved ones in the name of Jesus.

Yahweh, I know you want to work on me and bring healing to my family, restoration, and transformation to the lives of my children.

I know you have the power to move mountains, therefore, today, I rise in faith and humidity to cry out to you in Jesus's miraculous name.

Amen.

Weekly Reflection

Sometimes, we are reminded that pain and suffering are inevitable parts of the human experience. As Christians, we may face adversity in the form of an illness. Sickness has the potential to cripple us mentally, physically, and emotionally, but it can sometimes allow us to shift our emphasis away from our daily lives and toward God. Experiencing sickness may feel overwhelming or frightening, but it can also help us grow closer to God and strengthen our faith. Sometimes, God uses some of us best when we are weak and ill to perform something we could never have dreamed of.

As Christians, we are taught that when we are lost or feel weak, we should seek God and He will guide us on our journey. God is always with you and will help you carry your loads when they seem too heavy. God is all-powerful and has the ability to heal all diseases. Are you going through trials in the form of an illness? Maybe you have a loved one that is ill. How has this experience shaped your relationship with God?

How have you walked with Christ while you or a loved one has been ill? Have you walked by faith? What does it mean to walk by faith?

What should you do as a Christian when faced with a serious illness? What do you do to break the yoke of sickness? The Bible instructs us to prioritize prayer. God has the ability to break the yoke of sickness, but we must connect with Him. We must confess and bring our burdens to Him.

In (James 5:14), God says, "Is anyone among you sick? Let him call for the elders of the church, and let them pray over him, anointing him with oil in the name of the Lord." Write or say a prayer for yourself or a loved one that needs healing.

1ST DAY: BIBLE VERSE OF THE DAY: "And Jesus said to him, 'If you can! All things are possible for one who believes.'" (Mark 9:23).

Is there anything you need to change in your life as a result of reading this Bible verse?

2ND DAY: BIBLE VERSE OF THE DAY: "But Jesus on hearing this answered him, "do not fear; only believe, and she will be well." (Luke 8:5).

What have you learned from this Bible verse?

3RD DAY: BIBLE VERSE OF THE DAY: "But for you who fear my name, the sun of righteousness shall rise with healing in its wings. You shall go out leaping like calves from the stall." (Malachi 4:2).

Reflect on God's Word.

4TH DAY: BIBLE VERSE OF THE DAY: "Behold, I will bring to it health and healing, and I will heal them and reveal to them an abundance of prosperity and security." (Jeremiah 33:6).

Take a moment to invoke the name of Jesus to remove any illness that causes a tear in your flesh.

5TH DAY: BIBLE VERSE OF THE DAY: "He fulfills the desire of those who fear him; he also hears their cry and saves them." (Psalm 145:19).

What did you take out from this Bible verse?

6TH DAY: "For I will restore health to you, and your wounds I will heal, declares the Lord, because they have called you an outcast: 'It is Zion, for whom no one cares!'" (Jeremiah 30:17).

How does the message of this passage encourage deeper gratitude in Christ?

7TH DAY: Now, with the authority that God has given you, take a moment to rebuke any disease that the doctor has yet to detect, and it will not come near you in the great name of Jesus. Write or say a prayer to rid illness from you and your family.

BENEDICTION: "And the peace of God, which surpasses all understanding, will guard your hearts and your minds in Christ Jesus." (Philippians 4:7).

WEEK THIRTY: AN UPLIFTING PRAYER FOR MY CHILDREN

Dear Heavenly Father, the Creator of the universe, thank you for the precious gift of these amazing children. It's stated that children are gifts from the Lord.

I pray that every moment of their lives leads them on the right path. Keep them away from this corrupt world, the worldly influences, demonically inspired beliefs, cults, and the devil's trap.

Please, grant them the courage to believe in themselves and the insight to realize that what matters is how You view them, not what others think.
Always assist them in making the best decisions in life.

Give them the power to declare that they were born to be winners. They will always be the head, not the tail. Give them the knowledge to understand who they are in you.

Bless them with good, influential friends at school and on the university campus.
Help them to always arise and shine, so that everyone can contemplate your glory in them. Father, please, grant them good health and ensure that they lack nothing in life.
In the most precious name of Jesus Christ.
Amen.

Weekly Reflection

Praying for your children or grandchildren is essential.

If you don't have children, you can still pray for the youth in your family, church, or community.

Prayer for our children is extremely effective and rewarding.

When you pray, you place your child under the protection of the Most High and call on the angels to surround him or her, allowing God's power to touch his or her life.

Your knowledge, strength, and wisdom are insufficient, but God's might is limitless.

Are you having difficulties with your child or one of your children?

Perhaps your child is suffering from self-esteem issues. Maybe they are self-conscious about their appearance or their identity. Perhaps you have a youngster who is being influenced by a negative force in the world.

Without prayer, no matter how much time you devote to educating, teaching, training, and talking to your children, all of these vital things are futile. Today, make a commitment or a promise to teach and pray for your children every day. If you don't have a child, choose one or more children for whom you will pray every day for the rest of the year. Take an additional five minutes each day this week to lift your children to the Lord. You can choose to lift your grandchildren, nieces, nephews, godchildren, your neighbors' children, or the children from your church.

1ST DAY: BIBLE VERSE OF THE DAY: "And Jesus said to him, "If you can't all things are possible for one who believes." (Mark 9:23).

Jesus is powerful and can deliver your children from any hardship. Write or say a prayer dedicating your children to God and requesting God to keep them safe every day.

2ND DAY: BIBLE VERSE OF THE DAY: "Behold, children are a heritage from the LORD, the fruit of the womb a reward." (Psalm 127:3).

Write or say a prayer thanking God for your children.

3RD DAY: BIBLE VERSE OF THE DAY: "Do not be conformed to this world, but be transformed by the renewal of your mind, that by testing you may discern what is the will of God, what is good and acceptable and perfect." (Romans 12:2).

Write or say a prayer for strength for your children as they face negative influences of this world.

4TH DAY: BIBLE VERSE OF THE DAY: "Arise, shine, for your light has come, and the glory of the Lord has risen upon you." (Isaiah 60:1).

Write or say a prayer to God, requesting that He shine His light on your children.

5TH DAY: BIBLE VERSE OF THE DAY: "Be sober-minded; be watchful. Your adversary the devil prowls around like a roaring lion, seeking someone to devour." (1 Peter 5:8).

Write or say a prayer asking God to give your children the strength they need to battle the evil that may come their way.

6TH DAY: BIBLE VERSE OF THE DAY: "The Lord opens the eyes of the blind. The Lord lifts up those who are bowed down; the Lord loves the righteous." (Psalm 146:8).

Write or say a prayer asking God to open your children's minds to His teachings and to grant them spiritual sight if theirs is flawed and feeble.

7TH DAY: Reflect and speak words of blessings over your children now in the name of Jesus.

BENEDICTION: "The grace of the Lord Jesus Christ and the love of God and the fellowship of the Holy Spirit be with you all." (2 Corinthians 13:14).

WEEK THIRTY-ONE: AT YOUR WORD MIRACLES CAN HAPPEN

Most High God,

Be magnified Father! You reign forever. I lift up my hands before your throne as you are the King of kings, the Lion of the tribe of Judah, the Lamb of God.

I confess my sins and surrender everything to you. Today, I decided to cast my net in front of you to be filled.

Simon Peter from the Bible had struggled, felt frustrated, and was discouraged after fishing all night and catching nothing. At your Word, he surrendered, obeyed, and let down his nets and caught so many fishes that the net became too heavy for him to handle.

Now, I let down my empty nets, expecting a miracle from you.

Some of the nights are uncomfortable and long. Lord, I have had nightmares, experienced sleepless nights, turned from side to side, and worried about the problems with my life and my teenage children.

Please, help me to be obedient and let my nest down and trust in You. Thank you in advance for answering my prayer. I pray in the miraculous name of Jesus.

Amen.

Weekly Reflection

Have you ever experienced a personal miracle? Do you believe God still performs miracles? Do you think God can perform a miracle in your life if you cast your problems, stress, and anxiety on Him? God intervenes in our lives in unexpected ways. He helps us in ways we don't always see.

(Psalm 77:14) states that "You are the God who works wonders; you have made known your might among the peoples."

Everyday miracles occur all around us. However, many of us are often too preoccupied with our daily lives to notice them. Every day, we witness big and small miracles without knowing it. The ability to wake up and start a new day, for example, is a miracle. Another miracle is when a 10-month-old baby suddenly starts walking.

Another miracle is the ability to see and read. What are some of the everyday miracles you've witnessed in your daily life?

This week, give your worries to God and try to focus on the small and large miracles in your life. Write or say a prayer to God, thanking Him for small or big miracles in your life.

1ST DAY: BIBLE VERSE OF THE DAY: "Your word is a lamp to my feet and a light to my path." (Psalm 119:10).

Write or say a prayer placing all of your worries at Jesus's feet right now.

2ND DAY: BIBLE VERSE OF THE DAY: "The grass withers, the flower fades, but the worc of our God will stand forever." (Isaiah 40:8).

Write or say a prayer in which you entrust all of your troubles that you worry about day and night, to God.

3RD DAY: BIBLE VERSE OF THE DAY: "Simon answered, 'Master, we've worked hard all night and haven't caught anything. But because you say so, I will let down the nets.'" (Luke 5:5).

Do you have faith that if you trust God enough to let down your nets, He will accomplish a miracle in your life? Consider the last time you completely trusted God and let down your nets. When did that happen and what miracle did God perform in your life as a result?

4TH DAY: BIBLE VERSE OF THE DAY: "And the Lord will guide you continually and satisfy your desire in scorched places and make your bones strong; and you shall be like a watered garden, like a spring of water, whose waters do not fail." (Isaiah 58:11).

What does this Bible verse teach you about God?

5TH DAY: BIBLE VERSE OF THE DAY: "Delight yourself in the Lord, and he will give you the desires of your heart." (Psalm 37:4).

How will you spend the rest of the week delighting in God?

6TH DAY: BIBLE VERSE OF THE DAY: "He is the one you praise; he is your God, who performed for you those great and awesome wonders you saw with your own eyes." (Deuteronomy 10:21 NIV).

What is a personal miracle that has occurred in your life this year? One that strikes a chord with you.

7TH DAY: Be obedient to God. Whatever your net is today, lay it down at Jesus's feet and declare, in Jesus's name, that the impossible can become possible for you.

BENEDICTION: "And the peace of God, which surpasses all understanding, will guard your hearts and your minds in Christ Jesus." (Philippians 4:7).

WEEK THIRTY-TWO: "SPIRIT OF THE LIVING GOD FALL AFRESH ON ME"

Everlasting Father, Jehovah Rapha, and my Comforter,

You are my God; I worship you because You are the Holy Ghost baptizing.

The Advocate who stands and pleads with me in difficult moments. The Helper who lifts when the road of life seems slippery. Thank you for sending your Holy Spirit to give me strength against all sin.

I thank you for dwelling in my life. I invite you to renew my spirit and fill me anew.

Oh, Holy Father! Open my eyes so that I can see you and feel your presence. Holy Spirit revival comes from you and please send a revival now and baptize me fresh. Spirit of the Living God, you know without your presence I am weak, frail, and feel as if I am falling into a void. As such, please replenish me.

You performed this on the day of Pentecost for the disciples. They waited in one place and they were filled with the Holy Spirit. I am patiently waiting for the fire to consume every trace of iniquity and everything that is unlike you and transform my life to be like you. Please, grant me the spiritual fruit of patience. With you God, I am aware that when I am filled with sadness, it will transform into joy, my mourning into dancing, and my fear into courage. I want to set aside my egocentric ambition, jealousy, and immaturity.

Please, grant me the desire of my heart to walk in the spirit, to be empowered by the Holy Spirit, to live with the spirit, and produce the fruit of the spirit. Lord, anoint me so that others may see You and know you are God. I pray in the name of Jesus. Amen.

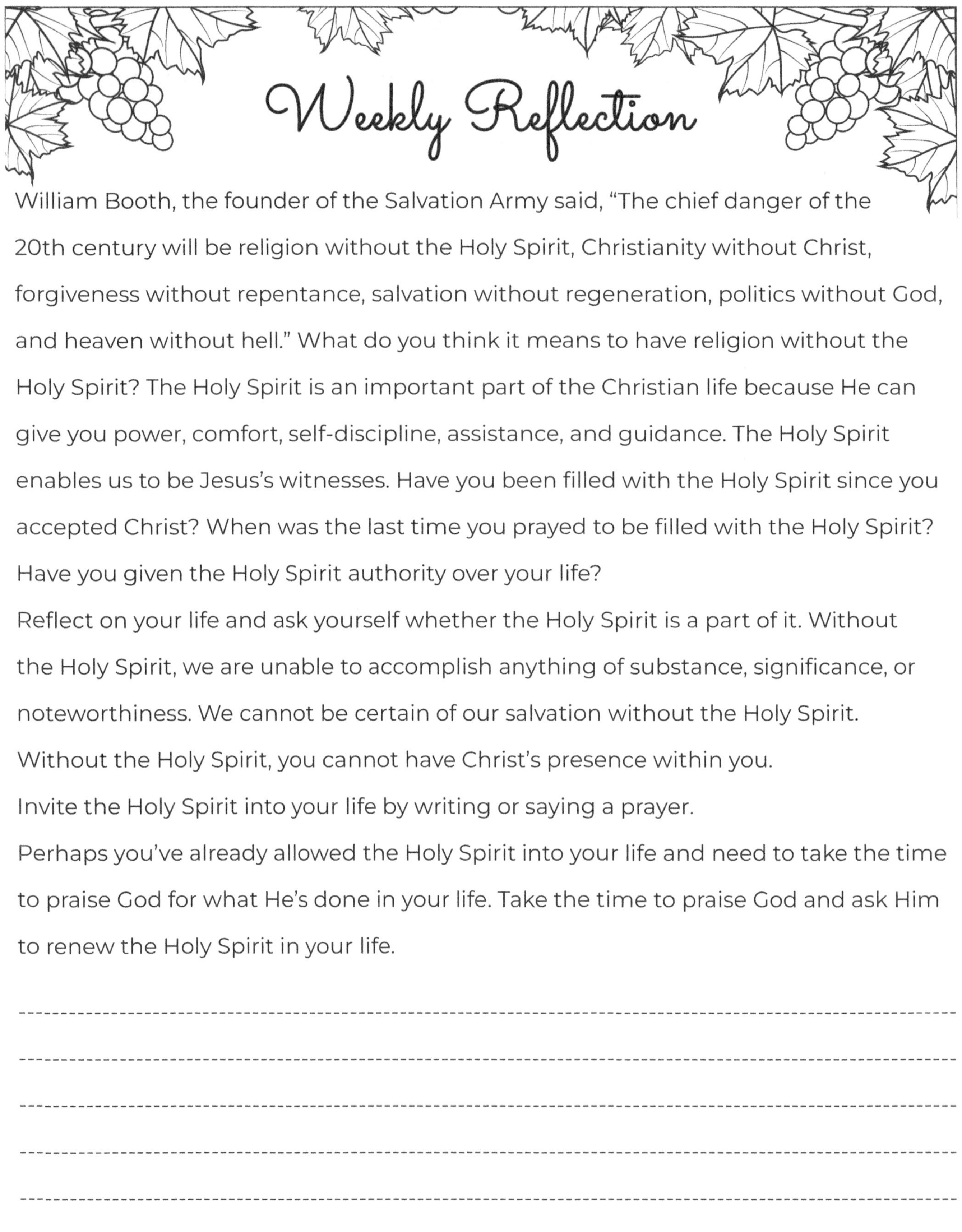

Weekly Reflection

William Booth, the founder of the Salvation Army said, “The chief danger of the 20th century will be religion without the Holy Spirit, Christianity without Christ, forgiveness without repentance, salvation without regeneration, politics without God, and heaven without hell.” What do you think it means to have religion without the Holy Spirit? The Holy Spirit is an important part of the Christian life because He can give you power, comfort, self-discipline, assistance, and guidance. The Holy Spirit enables us to be Jesus’s witnesses. Have you been filled with the Holy Spirit since you accepted Christ? When was the last time you prayed to be filled with the Holy Spirit? Have you given the Holy Spirit authority over your life?

Reflect on your life and ask yourself whether the Holy Spirit is a part of it. Without the Holy Spirit, we are unable to accomplish anything of substance, significance, or noteworthiness. We cannot be certain of our salvation without the Holy Spirit. Without the Holy Spirit, you cannot have Christ’s presence within you.

Invite the Holy Spirit into your life by writing or saying a prayer.

Perhaps you’ve already allowed the Holy Spirit into your life and need to take the time to praise God for what He’s done in your life. Take the time to praise God and ask Him to renew the Holy Spirit in your life.

1ST DAY: BIBLE VERSE OF THE DAY: "When the day of Pentecost arrived, they were all together in one place. And suddenly there came from heaven a sound like a mighty rushing wind, and it filled the entire house where they were sitting. And divided tongues as fire appeared to them and rested on each one of them. And they were all filled with the Holy Spirit and began to speak in other tongues as the Spirit gave them utterance." (Acts 2:1-4).

What does God want you to do after reading this passage?

2ND DAY: BIBLE VERSE OF THE DAY: "For our God is a consuming fire." (Hebrews 12:29)

Reflect on God's Word. What does it imply when God is described as a consuming fire?

3RD DAY: BIBLE VERSE OF THE DAY: "I baptize you with water for repentance, but he who is coming after me is mightier than I, whose sandals I am not worthy to carry. He will baptize you with the Holy Spirit and fire." (Matthew 3:11).

What does this Bible verse teach me about God?

4TH DAY: BIBLE VERSE OF THE DAY: "For the Lord your God is a consuming fire, a jealous God." (Deuteronomy 4:24).

How does this verse influence your views of God and your present circumstances?

5TH DAY: BIBLE VERSE OF THE DAY: "Nevertheless, I tell you the truth: it is to your advantage that I go away, for if I do not go away, the Helper will not come to you. But if I go, I will send him to you." (John 16:7).

Reflect on God's Word.

6TH DAY: BIBLE VERSE OF THE DAY: "The light of Israel will become a fire, and his Holy One a flame, and it will burn and devour his thorns and briers in one day." (Isaiah 10:17).

Reflect on God's Word.

7TH DAY: Spirit of the living God, I humbly bow down to you and ask you to fall afresh on me, fan the flame on me and seal me, mold me and fill me. Amen.

Write or say a prayer thanking God for the Holy Spirit.

BENEDICTION: "Finally, brethren, rejoice, be made complete, be comforted, be like minded, live in peace; and the God of love and peace will be with you."

(2 Corinthians 13:11).

WEEK THIRTY-THREE: I NEED A TURNAROUND IN MY LIFE

God, Heavenly Father,

How great you are O Lord! You deserve all glory and praise. I want to worship you as long as I live because You are Emmanuel, the Living God.

My name appears on the palms of your hands. You know everything about me, even my hair is numbered before you.

There is absolutely nothing that is impossible with you. Please, I just ask that you see me through these coming few weeks. I need a turnaround in my life. May I find a favor on your side. Even though my history is stained and ugly, you can change it. Thanks in advance for answering my prayer. I pray in the precious name of Jesus. Amen.

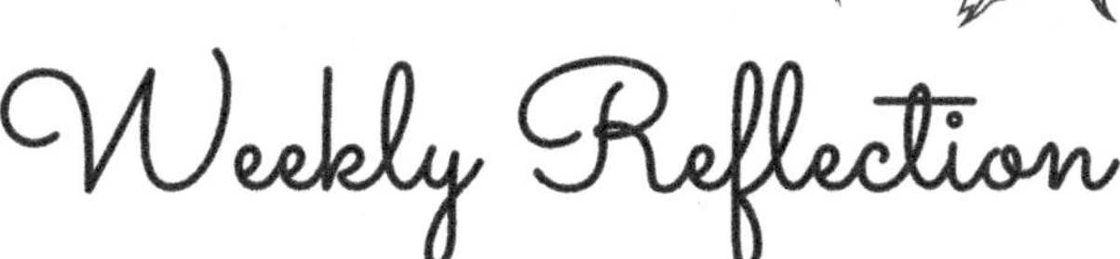

Weekly Reflection

Jesus did not die in vain. He saved the world and promised victory over the things of the world when He died for our sins. Christians always need to prepare themselves for a turnaround.

You may be wondering what a turnaround is. A turnaround is a change that occurs unexpectedly and improves things. When God intervenes, things must change, and our circumstances must have a turnaround.

The Bible has recorded so many turnarounds that occurred. For example, Jabez, whose name means pain, because of the pain he caused his mother during birth, cried to the Lord. He became the most honorable son. The widow and the prophet Elijah are two other examples. The former took her very small amount of oil and poured it into the first empty jar. Miraculously, the oil kept on pouring until the jar was filled. The story of Elijah being fed by ravens and the story of David fighting the giant Goliath and winning the battle because of God's help are all examples of turnaround that occurred in the Bible.

Have you come across a difficult situation that necessitates a turnaround? Perhaps your financial condition, family relationships, health, a habit, or your children's state of mind. What have you done to address this situation?

Have you brought the situation to God in prayer? Do you believe that God can turn impossible things around for you? While you look for a turnaround in your life, are you willing to obey God's command? No one should sit comfortably in his or her frustration and make excuses. Write or say a prayer crying out to God for a turnaround. He is masterful in how He handles everything in His time.

1ST DAY: BIBLE VERSE OF THE DAY: "Because you did not serve the Lord your God with joyfulness, and with gladness of heart, for the abundance of all things." (Deuteronomy 28:47).

God alone is worthy of our total surrender and dedication. What does it mean to submit to God? What does it entail to be in God's service?

2ND DAY: BIBLE VERSE OF THE DAY: "But godliness with contentment is great gain." (1 Timothy 6:6).

Have you found contentment and joy in what God has given you? How can you find happiness in God or continue to be contemptuous in your relationship with Christ?

3RD DAY: BIBLE VERSE OF THE DAY: "If we confess our sins, he is faithful to forgive our sins, and cleanse us from all unrighteousness." (John 1:9).

When was the last time you went to God and confessed your sins? Write or say a prayer to God acknowledging your sins in front of God.

4TH DAY: BIBLE VERSE OF THE DAY: "For those whom he foreknew he also predestined to be conformed to their image of his Son, in order that he might be the firstborn among many brothers." (Romans 8:29).

What do you believe God wants you to take away from this Bible verse?

5TH DAY: BIBLE VERSE OF THE DAY: "Blessed be the name of God forever and ever, to who belongs wisdom and might He changes times and seasons; He removes kings and sets up kings, he gives wisdom to the wise and knowledge to those who have understanding." (Daniel 2:20-21). Spend some time praying to God. Close your eyes, take a deep breath, picture God seated on His throne, and thank God for the knowledge and understanding that He provides you.

6TH DAY: "For I the Lord do not change; therefore you, O children of Jacob, are not consumed." (Malachi 3:6).

What does this Bible verse reveal to you?

7TH DAY: God's promise and purpose remain constant and unchangeable. Take some time to praise the Lord, who never changes.

What were some of the highlights of your week?

BENEDICTION: "And the peace of God, which surpasses all understanding, will guard your hearts and your minds in Christ Jesus." (Philippians 4:7).

WEEK THIRTY-FOUR: WELL/DESERT

The Most High God,

I worship You and adore You for You are the greatest. Yes, You are great and everything about You is great!

Thank you for always providing for me. You are the El Shadai, "The All-Sufficient God."

You helped Agard when she was helpless and in desperate need in the desert. She was hot, dusty, humid, and with no water, but Father, you didn't just provide her a little bit of water, but, a well appeared. How mighty you are! The well came about just in time for Agard and her son.

Everything is perfect in your time. You were on time for Agard. I believe that today is the day for my needs to be met by You.

I will not stay in the desert without water.

I won't stop crying before you until my well appears.

Thank you for always being there for me when I am in need. In Jesus's name,

Amen.

Weekly Reflection

When you think of the desert, what do you envision? I've never been to a desert, but I've crossed over the Sahara several times while traveling by plane between Europe and Africa. Some years ago, I was traveling from Brazzaville, Congo, going to London, England, with a layover in Morocco. On that trip, I felt as if I had a little experience of the desert. To get to our destination, we had to cross the Sahara.

I was not aware that we were approaching because I tend to sleep and pray on long flights. The plane ride became very bumpy and the temperature became hot inside while crossing. I was perplexed and had no idea what was going on until one of the flight attendants informed us that we were crossing the Sahara and asked us to be patient! I took the time to pray.

A desert is typically a very dry place with weather that varies from day to night.

I envision a desert devoid of trees, full of sand and dust, hot and sticky, with the sun beating down from a cloudless sky.

Consider everything you know about the desert, and then read (Genesis 21:15-20) to learn about the story of Hagar and her son and their experience in the Desert of Beersheba. The story of Hagar and her son wandering through the desert until they ran out of water is told in the Bible. Imagine what it would be like to run out of water while wandering around a desert. Hagar reached a point in her life when she felt it was her final moment and began to weep. As Hagar waited for her son to die in the desert, she had a moment of despair. Then the God who sees intervenes on her behalf. Even in the midst of chaos, God sees us. It makes no difference what your current situation, past experience, or mistakes are, God sees us. During our difficulties, God sees us.

Have you ever reached a stage in your life when you thought it was your last? What happened to put you in that position? How did you deal with that situation? Did you seek Him when you thought it was your final moment?

God is present and aware of our situation. Hagar's eyes were opened by God to see the well in the middle of the desert. Is your life pleasing to God? Are you prepared to see your own well in the desert?

Have you ever prayed to God to open your spiritual eyes so you can see your well in the desert? Write or say a prayer to God, asking Him to spiritually open your eyes to see your well in the middle of the desert.

1ST DAY: BIBLE VERSE OF THE DAY: "With joy you will draw water from the wells of salvation." (Isaiah 12:3).

Are you drawing from the wells of Salvation? Reflect on your experience and continue to keep your gaze fixed on Him.

2ND DAY: BIBLE VERSE OF THE DAY: "Believe in me, as the Scripture has said, Out of his heart will flow rivers of living water." (John 7:38).

Take a moment to write or say a prayer asking God to help you be persistent in your faith.

3RD DAY: BIBLE VERSE OF THE DAY: "And God heard the voice of the boy, and the angel of God called to Hagar from heaven and said to her. What troubles you, Hagar? Fear not, for God has heard the voice of the boy where he is." (Genesis 21:17).

The Lord showed Hagar and her son favor in the desert. Write or utter a petition to God for favor in your life.

4TH DAY: BIBLE VERSE OF THE DAY: "For I will pour water on the thirsty land, and streams on the dry ground; I will pour my Spirit upon your offspring, and my blessing on your descendants." (Isaiah 44:3).

Reflect on God's Words.

5TH DAY: BIBLE VERSE OF THE DAY: "I will sprinkle clean water on you, and you shall be clean from all uncleanliness, and from all your idols I will cleanse you."
(Ezekiel 36:25).
Take a moment to praise God for bringing you to this point and for making you whole and clean. If you are not where you need to be, ask God to make you whole and cleanse you of all uncleanness.

6TH DAY: BIBLE VERSE OF THE DAY: "But Whoever drinks the water that I will give him will never be thirsty again. The water that I will give him will become in him a spring of water welling up to eternal life." (John 4:14).
After reading this Bible verse, what is one action you should take today?

7TH DAY: Keep praying and believing that in the midst of struggle, blessings can appear, life can change, and problems can be solved. Claim the spiritual well that God has prepared somewhere for you. Thank God for opening your spiritual eyes to see the blessings that are in store for you.

BENEDICTION: "And God is able to bless you abundantly, so that in all things at all times, having all that you need, you will abound in every good work" I ask all these in the name of a king of kings and Lord." (2 Corinthians 9:8).

WEEK THIRTY-FIVE: A PRAYER FOR SPIRITUAL AUTHORITY

Dear Heavenly Father, the Creator,

You are the author of Salvation. You are Blessed Redeemer. I want to raise and shout "Hallelujah!" And let the whole world know that you are mighty, the Comforter, and the Holy Ghost.

I want to use the authority you've given me to good use and stop living in a victim mentality. I know every day you renew my strength. O Lord, anoint me with the power to speak words of safety over my life, over my children's lives, and the lives of my family. I am confident that your Spirit is on me. I proclaim a life of the Lord's favor over my family, to stop the enemy attack, to declare freedom over iron gates that blocked my way.

Today, I claim the blood of Jesus daily covers my life, my husband, my children, and my grandchildren's lives.

Please, Yahweh, help me in surrendering to you, as I am aware that my spiritual power will come when I fully surrender to you.

I say thank you, father, for all your goodness. In Jesus' name, I pray.

Amen.

Weekly Reflection

What is the significance of power and authority? People battle for authority and power in order to be in control, change things to suit their own agenda, and achieve their personal goals. Individuals throughout the world kill, imprison, steal from others, or declare war in order to gain power.

However, few people seek the power that Jesus provides, which is far greater than the power that the world provides. Jesus stated, "Behold, I have given you authority to tread on serpents and scorpions, and over all the power of the enemy, and nothing shall hurt you" (Luke 10:19). What a beautiful promise to know that we have power over our adversary who wishes to harm our lives. We have the power to overcome our feelings of inferiority and live a life that is pleasing to God as well as be His witness to others. Every Christian should exercise their authority.

Do you lead a life in which you feel powerless? You feel powerless with no authority no matter what you do. Perhaps you have people in your life who regularly impose their authority and control over you. What do you think causes you to feel powerless? What are some of the emotions you experience when you feel powerless?

At times, you may feel powerless, but if you believe in Him, His power is at work in you, and that gives you the power you need. Do not forget that as Christians, we have God's omnipotence inside us and must rely on the Holy Spirit to give us the power to serve the Lord and live a life pleasing to Him. If you are feeling powerless, you need to turn to Jesus because you have spiritual authority in Christ. Do you understand the spiritual authority that you possess? Write or say a prayer and ask the Lord to assist you in establishing yourself as a spiritual authority in your life and family.

1ST DAY: BIBLE VERSE OF THE DAY: "But they who wait for the Lord shall renew their strength; they shall mount up with wings like eagles; they shall run and not be weary; they shall walk and not faint." (Isaiah 40:31).

Have you ever prayed 'the scripture'? You might be wondering what it means to pray 'the scripture'. I feel that the most powerful prayers are those that are directly from God's Word. Praying the scripture is converting the scripture into a prayer. Write or say a prayer using God's Words from this Bible verse.

2ND DAY: BIBLE VERSE OF THE DAY: "Wait for the Lord, be strong, and let your heart take courage; wait for the Lord!" (Psalm 27:14).

Reflect on God's Words.

3RD DAY: BIBLE VERSE OF THE DAY: "I wait for the Lord my soul waits and in his word I hope." (Psalm 130:5).

Let us take a few seconds to listen to the Lord. What does the Bible say to you today? Write or say a prayer to the Divine Helper asking for patience.

4TH DAY: BIBLE VERSE OF THE DAY: "Be strong, and let your heart take courage, all you who wait for the Lord." (Psalm 31:24).

Reflect on His Words.

5TH DAY: BIBLE VERSE OF THE DAY: "In the path of your judgments, O Lord, we wait for you; your name and remembrance are the desire of our soul." (Isaiah 26:8).

Take the time to study God's Word. What did the Holy Spirit reveal to you in this verse?

6TH DAY: BIBLE VERSE OF THE DAY: "Be still before the Lord wait patiently for Him; fret not yourself over the one who prospers in his way, over the man who carries out evil devices." (Psalm 37:7).

What does this Bible verse teach you?

7TH DAY: What has been on your mind this week?

Spend the next 10 to 15 minutes praying in silence, waiting for God to speak to you.

BENEDICTION: "The LORD bless you and keep you; the LORD make his face to shine upon you and be gracious to you; the LORD lift up his countenance upon you and give you peace." (Numbers 6:24-26).

WEEK THIRTY-SIX: A PRAYER FOR ALL WOMEN IN SOCIETY

Father God in heaven, the Creator of the Universe,
I come to you thanking you for your great love for me. Lord, I come to you to pray for the women in my family, my church, and my community. Lord, I pray for all of the women that continually make a positive difference in society. Being a woman in this society can be difficult at times. Some women face discrimination, are oppressed, and are treated as second-class citizens.

During your earthly mission, the Samaritans, women, and others were treated as outcasts, yet, you never showed favoritism to anyone. You love us equally.
In the Bible, you showed favor to Rabab the prostitute, the Samaritan woman, and the woman who washed your feet with perfume. We all belong to you. According to your Word, we are all one in Christ Jesus.
Thank you so much, Lord.

O Lord, now I pray for women who feel inferior, neglected, and rejected as a result of culture, tradition, or a failed relationship.

I pray for the victims of gender-based violence, as well as those who are prevented from owning property as a result of the law of their land and social conventions.

Oh Lord, have mercy on these women. I claim liberty for women who can't make any decisions about their own lives. Have mercy O Lord! I declare victory for women whose legal rights are almost nonexistent. Have mercy O Lord! I claim equal pay for equal work for all working women in the name of Jesus. Have mercy O Lord!

I pray that you delete and erase any notions of a glass ceiling for minorities and eliminate the discriminatory gender gap in the workplace. Have mercy O Lord! I pray that bigotry and inequality be eradicated. Have mercy O Lord! Please intervene on their behalf. I pray in the mighty name of Jesus.

Amen.

Weekly Reflection

Women are God's gifts to mankind. Let us face it: without women, the planet would perish. Yet, women are treated as second-class citizens in many regions of the world. Many women have no rights in some places around the world.

Depending on where you are currently living, you might think this is a non-issue. You might say that women are treated equally where I reside. I respectfully disagree because women have many rights but are not always treated equally, as evidenced by pay disparities. Many women are paid less than men for performing the same tasks. Some women are still discriminated against in the workplace, and men are sometimes given preferential treatment in specific fields.

Some may argue that men ruled society in the past, especially during the time of the Bible. The Bible, on the other hand, makes no suggestion that women are inferior to men. Jesus never discriminated against women. For Christ, women have equal value. Women and men were both created in the image of God. Both men and women have personal freedom, and a measure of self-determination. We may have different roles at times, but it does not mean that women are less valuable than men. When Jesus was arrested, and crucified, it was women, His devoted followers of Jesus, who went to attend to His body. It was women who first witnessed Jesus's resurrection God does not have a preference and we are equal ambassadors of God. What do you think it means to be a woman of God? Based on your definition, are you a woman of God? Are you an ambassador for God? What can you do to support a woman in your family, place of employment, church, or community? Write or say a prayer for a woman in your family, community, or church. Lift the person to God in prayer.

1ST DAY: BIBLE VERSE OF THE DAY: "Yes, I ask you also, true companion, help these women, who have labored side by side with me in the gospel together with Clement and the rest of my fellow workers, whose names are in the book of life. Rejoice in the Lord always; again I will say, rejoice." (Philippians 4:3-4).

Let God's Word speak to you today. What did the Holy Spirit reveal to you in this verse?

2ND DAY: BIBLE VERSE OF THE DAY: "And David said to Abigail, 'Blessed be the Lord, the God of Israel, who sent you this day to meet me! Blessed be your discretion, and blessed be you, who have kept me this day from bloodguilt and from working salvation with my own hand!'" (1 Samuel 25:32-33).

What are your thoughts after reading this Bible verse? How are you currently feeling?

3RD DAY: BIBLE VERSE OF THE DAY: "Every good gift and every perfect gift is from above, coming down from the Father of light with whom there is no variation or shadow due to change." (James 1:17).

Read the Bible verse a few times and listen to God's voice today. Write or say a prayer thanking God for all of His gifts from above.

4TH DAY: BIBLE VERSE OF THE DAY: "For I know the plans I have for you,' declares the Lord, 'plans to prosper you and not to harm you, plans to give you hope and a future.'" (Jeremiah 29:11 NIV).

God has a plan for your life. How do you know God's plan for your life? You can tell if you are following God's plan for your life by praying. Spending time each day thinking about the Lord and He will assist you in learning His plans for you. Spend a moment in prayer with Jesus.

5TH DAY: BIBLE VERSE OF THE DAY: "And Mary said: 'Behold, I am the servant of the Lord; let it be to me according to your word. And the angel departed from her.'" (Luke 1:38).

Reflect on God's Word.

6TH DAY: BIBLE VERSE OF THE DAY: "But on the first day of the week, at early dawn, they went to the tomb, taking the spices they had prepared. And they found the stone rolled away from the tomb, but when they went in they did not find the body of the Lord Jesus Christ. While they were perplexed about this, two men stood by them in dazzling apparel. And as they were frightened and bowed their faces to the ground, the men said to them, 'why do you seek the living among the dead?'" (Luke 24:1-5 NIV). What does this Bible verse tell you about God?

7TH DAY: As a woman who is a Christian, what are you thankful for God today?

BENEDICTION: "The Lord bless you and keep you; the Lord make his face to shine upon you and be gracious to you; The Lord lifts up his countenance upon you and give you peace." (Numbers 6:24).

WEEK THIRTY-SEVEN: PRAYER FOR THE PROCLAMATION OF POWER IN THE NAME OF JESUS

Mighty Savior, I bow down before your powerful name, the name which is above every name. The name that God exalted to the highest place. The name that every knee should bow in heaven and on earth and under the earth, the name that every tongue acknowledges that you are Lord.

So, I call upon your great name, because I know there is healing in Your name, there is deliverance in Your name. There is power in the name of Jesus. There is restoration, there is peace, there is satisfaction and yes, there is freedom in the name of Jesus. Father, I know sickness and demons can flee the body, and those who are paralyzed can walk, all in your name.

Lord, you do not want me to lose the battle. Sickness does not belong to my body. My marriage is until death do us part, and my children will be successful in seeking higher education and have a fulfilling career. You stated that if we believe, we will see the glory of God. So, I believe in the most precious name of Jesus Christ, the Everlasting Father, I am confident that everything will come true. I pray in the name of Jesus.

Amen

Weekly Reflection

During pregnancy, expectant parents have a lot of decisions to make, and one of those decisions is deciding on a name for their child. The name of a person has huge significance and in some cases consequences. For example, people might make assumptions about a person simply based on their name.

For this reason, some parents find naming their child stressful, while others find it enjoyable and look to be creative, then you find parents who have approached the task in unusual ways.

Do you remember how you selected the names of your children if you have any? Did you simply peruse a book or website and read through names until you discovered one that piqued your interest? Perhaps the names you and your husband chose were those of your grandparents or other members of your family.

Maybe the names you chose for your children have special meanings. What about you, do you have a story about your name? Maybe there is a special meaning behind your name. How do you feel about your name? Take a moment to reflect.

Names were laden with meaning, hope, and assumption during the period of the Bible and this is still the case in some families now.

The names of people described in biblical stories had enormous value and provided hope. Among all the names in the Bible, the name of Jesus stands out as the most powerful. The name of Jesus is magnificent, and dignified. There is something special about the name of Jesus.

(Philippians 2:9) says, "Therefore God has highly exalted him and bestowed on him the name that is above every name."

The name of Jesus is so powerful that a Christian can accomplish miracles and renounce the devil in His name. Do you believe that the name of Jesus possesses power? When was the last time you invoked Jesus's name? Reflect on the last time you used the name of Jesus. What happened when you called the name of Jesus?

1ST DAY: BIBLE VERSE OF THE DAY: "And these signs will accompany those who believe: In my name they will drive out demons; they will speak in new tongues; they will pick up snakes with their hands; and when they drink deadly poison, it will not hurt them at all; they will place their hands on sick people, and they will get well." (Mark 16:17-18).

What are your thoughts about these verses, what does God reveal through His Word?

2ND DAY: BIBLE VERSE OF THE DAY: "And there is salvation in no one else, for there is no other name under heaven given among men by which we must be saved." (Acts 4:12).

Reflect on the Words of God.

3RD DAY: BIBLE VERSE OF THE DAY: "Whatever you ask in my name, this I will do, that the Father may be glorified in the Son, if you ask me anything in my name, I will do it." (John 14:13-14).

Take the time to proclaim the name of Jesus and claim victory.

4TH DAY: BIBLE VERSE OF THE DAY: "If you ask me anything in my name, I will do it." (John 14:14).

What do you wish to ask God in His name? Do you want to write or speak a prayer requesting God to do something special in His name? Take a moment to do so.

5TH DAY: BIBLE VERSE OF THE DAY: "And whatever you do, in word or deed, do everything in the name of the Lord Jesus, giving thanks to God the Father through him." (Colossians." 3:17).

Take a moment to give God thanks for all He has done for you this year so far.

6TH DAY: BIBLE VERSE OF THE DAY: "The seventy-two returned with joy, saying, 'Lord, even the demons are subject to us in your name!'" (Luke 10:17).

Reflect on God's Words.

7TH DAY: Now, using Jesus's name, claim a miracle for yourself.

BENEDICTION: "And the peace of God, which surpasses all understanding, will guard your hearts and your minds in Christ Jesus." (Philippians 4:7).

WEEK THIRTY-EIGHT: A PRAYER FOR MOTHER'S DAY

Sovereign Lord,

We approach before your throne at this moment to thank you for mothers in the whole world. They are special to us. We thank You for creating them with all kinds of gifts, talents, wisdom, and patience.

How can we ever repay them for the sacrifice they make during pregnancy, spending time in the labor room, and sleepless nights? We thank you for the strength and endurance you gave them to take care of us from babies, toddlers, and school-age to mature adults.

Nevertheless, the work is never done. Her continual prayers, her love, and her kindness will continue till the end of her days.

As we celebrate Mother's Day today, we claim a special outpouring of the Holy Spirit to pour a flood of blessings upon every one of them. Today, we want to pray for single moms, hurting moms, disappointed moms, sick moms, potential moms battling infertility, moms with special needs of children, and potential moms who constantly have miscarriages. Please, have mercy upon them.

We pray for mothers who are addicted to something or other, for those who have used and abused their children. Lord, have pity upon them. We pray for mothers who felt they had no choice but to put their children up for adoption because of some challenges. Please, Yahweh, extend your mighty hands of compassion and grace over each one of them.

Thank you, Father, for seeing them in your love and companion that never fails.

I ask for all these mercies in the most precious name of Jesus Christ our Savior.

Amen.

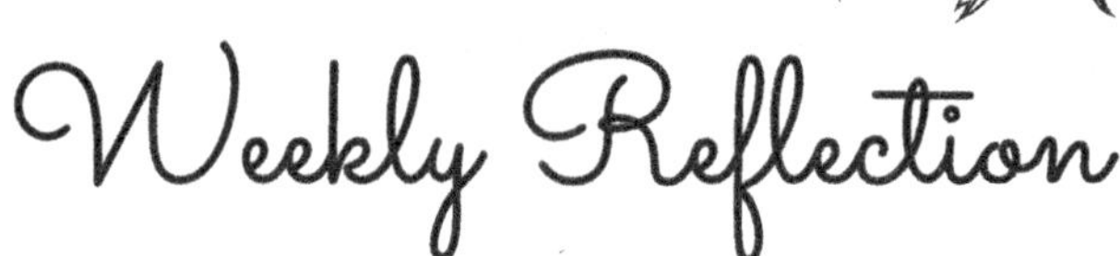

Weekly Reflection

Mother's Day is always a wonderful occasion for many of us because it allows us not only to express gratitude for our moms, but maybe also the time to contemplate the mothering aspects of our God. A good mother is a representation of God, inspiring kindness and self-sacrifice.

We can feel God's love in the way our mother loves us or hugs us. A mother is a sign of God's presence. God's love for us is illustrated by the image of a mother comforting her child. From before we were even born, God loved us and cared for us like a mother would.

What are some of the characteristics of a good mother? What are the qualities of a Christian mother? Do you possess any of those characteristics? Do you think some of the characteristics of a good and Christian mother have some similarities with the characteristics of Jesus?

How do you react when your children make a mistake? Do you have any less affection for them? What is Jesus's reaction when you do something wrong? Do you believe God loves you less when you make a mistake or do something wrong? God loves you regardless of how well or poorly you behave. Take some time to pray and meditate on His Words. Mothers are delighted to spend time with their children, just imagine how much more delighted Jesus is to spend time with us, His children. Take some time and spend it with God.

1ST DAY: BIBLE VERSE OF THE DAY: "Her children rise up and call her blessed; her husband also, and he praises her: 'Many women have done excellently, but you surpass them all.'" (Proverbs 31:28-29).

Reflect on God's Words.

2ND DAY: BIBLE VERSE OF THE DAY: "Honor your father and your mother, that your days may be long in the land that the Lord your God is giving you." (Exodus 20:12).

What do you think it means in the Bible to honor your mother?

3RD DAY: BIBLE VERSE OF THE DAY: "As one whom his mother comforts, so I will comfort you; you shall be comforted in Jerusalem." (Isaiah 66:13).

God will bring His people the kind of comfort that only a mother can give.

Has there ever been a time in this month when you needed God's comfort?

How has God helped you feel better over the past month?

4TH DAY: BIBLE VERSE OF THE DAY: "Give her of the fruit of her hands, and let her works praise her in the gates." (Proverbs 31:31).

What does this Bible verse teach me?

5TH DAY: BIBLE VERSE OF THE DAY: "When Jesus, therefore, saw his mother and the disciple standing by, whom he loved, he saith unto his mother, woman, behold thy son! Then he said to the disciple, Behold thy mother! And from that hour that disciple took her unto his own home." (John 19:27-28).

Reflect on God's Word.

6TH DAY: BIBLE VERSE OF THE DAY: "Then the mother of the child said, 'As the Lord lives and as you yourself live, I will not leave you.' So He arose and followed Her." (2 Kings 4:30).

Reflect on God's Word.

7TH DAY: I'd like to thank all of the mothers who have read and prayed the prayers in this book; I love and appreciate you. You are extremely valuable in the eyes of God. Take a few moments to write or say a prayer of thanksgiving to God.

BENEDICTION: "And the peace of God, which surpasses all understanding, will guard your hearts and your minds in Christ Jesus." (Philippians 4:7).

WEEK THIRTY-NINE: A PRAYER FOR INNER PEACE IN MY FAMILY

Everlasting Father, Jehovah Shalom,

I glorify your name because you are worthy to be praised! Today, Lord, may you bring peace to my house according to your Word. When I lie down, I will not be afraid. When I lie down, I will sleep in sweet peace.

May my house become a shelter where my family rests under Your shadow. I know that you will cover each person that abides in this house as a hen covers his cheeks. Your Word teaches us in (Psalms 91) that if I make the Most High my dwelling, no hardship will overtake me, and no disease will come near my tent. Thank you, Lord. Father, may the walls of my house know nothing of sadness, bitterness, or quarrel. May it be a house filled with your presence. May your Spirit abide and fall afresh on every one of us.

May your holy angel encamp around every corner of this house so that the tireless spirit cannot have access to harm us.

Keep us safe, Father, because we take refuge in you. You are our Lord, and we have nothing good apart from you. I know you will keep us in perfect peace. Thank you for answering our prayers. In the mighty name of Jesus.

Amen.

Weekly Reflection

Our society is marked by upheaval, instability, natural disasters, and discontent. Many wish for peace. In many families, the worst problems, abuse, quarrels, and wrath are exhibited. Many people, however, want peace in their community and the world, as well as harmony in their homes. They want freedom from drama, issues, and commotion. Many people also seek God's peace when they have no lasting comfort or freedom in their lives.

Only God can provide true peace. (John 14:27) states, "Peace I leave with you; my peace I give to you. Not as the world gives do I give to you. Let not your hearts be troubled, neither let them be afraid." Do you have any tension at home right now? Are you under constant stress at home or in your family?
How can God bring you peace in your home and your family? (Colossians 3:13) states, "Bear with each other and forgive one another if any of you has a grievance against someone. Forgive as the Lord forgave you."

Write or say a prayer now, asking God to help you with knowledge, direction, the Spirit of discernment, and serenity. Take the time to pray for compassion and for words that will bless you and your family rather than hurt you.

1ST DAY: BIBLE VERSE OF THE DAY: "Peace I leave with you; my peace I give to you. Not as the world gives do I give to you. Let not your hearts be troubled, neither let them be afraid." (John 14:27).

Reflect on God's Word.

2ND DAY: BIBLE VERSE OF THE DAY: "I have said these things to you, that in me you may have peace. In the world you will have tribulation. But take heart; I have overcome the world." (John 16:33).

Do you have inner peace, if not, maybe write or say a prayer to God asking Him for inner peace.

3RD DAY: BIBLE VERSE OF THE DAY: "Blessed are the peacemakers, for they shall be called sons of God." (Matthew 5:9).

As Christians, we should strive to be peacemakers and slow to anger. Are you a peacemaker? How could God use you as a peacemaker in your family or church?

4TH DAY: BIBLE VERSE OF THE DAY: "And they said, 'Believe in the Lord Jesus, and you will be saved, you and your household.'" (Deuteronomy 6:6-7).

After reading this verse, what does God want you to do or believe?

5TH DAY: BIBLE VERSE OF THE DAY: "How good and pleasant it is when God's people live together in unity!" (Psalm 133:1).

Reflect on God's Words.

6TH DAY: BIBLE VERSE OF THE DAY: "A friend loves at all times, and a brother is born for adversity." (Proverbs 17:17).

What does this Bible verse reveal to you? Take a moment to thank God for His love and peace.

7TH DAY: BIBLE VERSE OF THE DAY: "The God of peace will soon crush Satan under your feet. The grace of our Lord Jesus be with you." (Romans 16:20).

Write or say a prayer thanking God for His grace.

BENEDICTION: "Finally, brethren, rejoice, be made complete, be comforted, be like-minded, live in peace; and the God of love and peace will be with you."

(2 Corinthians 11:13).

WEEK FORTY: I AM A CONQUEROR IN THE NAME OF THE LORD

Mighty Savior, the King of kings, the Lord of lords,

I come before you in humble adoration to thank you for what you have done for me and what you will continue to do. I worship you and praise you. You have done great things, so I want to bless your holy name. You are in heaven, but you rule over all the earth. What a powerful God you are. You established your throne in the heavens, and your sovereignty rules over all.

Regardless of what is going on in the world, I know I am an overcomer. With this great assurance, I refuse to complain about my situation. I decided to change my attitude. I ask you to visit me and take me out of this spirit of imprisonment that always tells me day after day that I am a victim. May your Spirit abide in me to remind me daily that I am a warrior, a conqueror in the name of the Lord.

Thank you for liberating me from bitterness and transforming me into a people warrior, fighter, determiner, and conqueror. I know if I am going through a trial, I can put my hope in You, the mighty God. I declare today that I am a winner.

I pray in the powerful name of Jesus.

Amen.

Weekly Reflection

What is the definition of a conqueror? I describe a conqueror as a fighter, someone who stands up to what is wrong, someone who is a winner and victorious.

What is your definition of the word conqueror? Do you consider yourself a conqueror?

"No, in all these things we are more than conquerors through him who loved us," Paul wrote in (Romans 8 verse 37). Paul wrote this to encourage Christians to stand firm in faith in times of persecution, hardship, famine, nakedness, difficulties, and sword—stand in faith and conviction because victory is on the way. When God is with us, we will be more than conquerors. To be more than conquerors means to face life's hardships with the assurance that we are not alone. We have a God who is fighting for us.(Psalm 46:2-3) states, "Therefore we will not fear though the earth gives way, though the mountains be moved into the heart of the sea, though its waters roar and foam, though the mountains tremble at its swelling."

Write or say a prayer asking God to be more than a conqueror.

1ST DAY: BIBLE VERSE OF THE DAY: "For the Lord, your God is he who goes with you to fight for you against your enemies, to give you the victory." (Deuteronomy 20:4).

Reflect on God's Word.

2ND DAY: BIBLE VERSE OF THE DAY: "I have said these things to you, that in me you may have peace. In the world you will have tribulation, but take heart; I have overcome the world." (John 16:33).

God has called you to a magnificent life made possible by Jesus's victory over death and sin.

Write or say a prayer of thanksgiving.

3RD DAY: BIBLE VERSE OF THE DAY: "The Lord is not slow to fulfill his promise as some count slowness, but is patient toward you, not wishing that any should perish, but that all should reach repentance." (2 Peter 3:9).

What does God want you to believe after reading His Words?

4TH DAY: BIBLE VERSE OF THE DAY: “Finally, be strong in the Lord and in the strength of his might.” (Ephesians 6:10).

Take a moment to reflect on God’s Word.

5TH DAY: BIBLE VERSE OF THE DAY: “Salvation belongs to the Lord; your blessing be on your people.” (Psalm 3:8).

What do you think it means that "Salvation belongs to the Lord?"

6TH DAY: BIBLE VERSE OF THE DAY: “What then shall we say to these things? If God is for us, who can be against us? He who did not spare his own Son gave him up for us all, how will he not also with him graciously give us all things.” (Romans 8:31-32).

Reflect on God’s Word and lift up your needs of the day.

7TH DAY: Praise, prayer, and thanksgiving:

BENEDICTION: "And the peace of God, which surpasses all understanding, will guard your hearts and your minds in Christ Jesus." (Philippians 4:7).

WEEK FORTY-ONE: I NEED A CHANGE IN MY LIFE

Dear God, O Lord Almighty,

I bless your holy name and worship you with reverence and humility.

You are the King of all kings. You are the one upon whom I lay my worries, which weigh heavily on my existence. I am confident that You will intervene on my behalf.

You have helped Jabez, who experienced identity issues. He refused to remain the way he was born. He rejected the negative connotation of his name.

You, Lord, altered his condition, instead of allowing him to continue suffering, and misery. He became the most honorable. You will do the same for me. You created me in Your image and You love me.

Please, Lord, I need a change in my current life situation. Lord, sculpt and shape me to become more like you. I ask all these mercies in your Son's name.

Amen.

Weekly Reflection

We all go through life-changing experiences. Sometimes, it's only for a specific time of day or a series of events that occur over a period of time. Some of the life-changing events are positive, while others can be upsetting. Many of us might be wanting or praying for a life-changing event. We are in a situation where we feel the need for change. How can you tell when you need a change in your life? Is there anything going on in your life to make you understand that you need to make a change?

God has the ability to change anything and improve our situation. He is capable of doing what must be accomplished. He can make things better when we put our trust in Him. If you want to make a change in your life, having a relationship with God can give you the courage and strength to do so.

What do you need God to do in your life today? How badly do you want Him to alter your life?

1ST DAY: BIBLE VERSE OF THE DAY: "The LORD is my strength and my song, and he has become my salvation; this is my God, and I will praise him, my father's God, and I will exalt him." (Exodus 15:2).

Reflect on God's Word.

2ND DAY: BIBLE VERSE OF THE DAY: "And God raised the Lord and will also raise us up by his power." (1 Corinthians 6:14).

Take the time to meditate on God's Word. What did the Holy Spirit reveal to you in this verse?

3RD DAY: BIBLE VERSE OF THE DAY: "For everything there is a season, and a time for every matter under heaven." (Ecclesiastes 3:1).

Today, ask God to give you patience while you wait on Him for a new season.

4TH DAY: BIBLE VERSE OF THE DAY: "But for you, O Lord, do I wait; it is you, O Lord my God, who will answer. For I said, 'Only let them not rejoice over me, who boast against me when my foot slips!' for I am ready to fall, and my pain is ever before me.

I confess my iniquity; I am sorry for my sin." (Psalm 38:15-18).

Let these Bible verses speak to you today.

5TH DAY: BIBLE VERSE OF THE DAY: "For the word of God is living and active, sharper than any two-edged sword, piercing to the division of soul and of spirit, of joints and of marrow, and discerning the thoughts and intentions of the heart." (Hebrew 4:12).

What steps must be taken to live according to the truths of His Words?

6TH DAY: BIBLE VERSE OF THE DAY: "For God gave us a spirit not of fear but of power and love and self-control." (2 Timothy 1:7).

Fears can rob us of many things in our life. It can rob us of our power and occasionally bring us down. Write or say a prayer thanking God for the power of love and self-contro

----

7TH DAY: Jesus the Lamb of God and the King of kings, you are high on your throne above. I cry out to you in my pain. I ask that you hold me back from anguish, animosity, and revulsion. In the glorious name of Jesus Christ, Amen. Take a moment to cry out to the Lord for your blessings.

BENEDICTION: "The Lord bless you and keep you; the Lord makes his face shine upon you and be gracious to you; The Lord lifts up his countenance upon you and gives you peace." (Numbers 6:24).

WEEK FORTY-TWO: GOD WATCHES OVER ME

Mighty God and my Protector, the True and only Living God,

I come before your throne of grace again today to thank you for the authority and protection you have given me. As your daughter, I drive every day with the assurance that the host of angels is watching over me and my family. With so many irresponsible and negligent drivers on the road, the road is extremely dangerous. I ask that you keep myself and my family safe by surrounding us with your gentle care. I know you keep an eye on me all hours of the day and night. You never slumber nor sleep.

Surely, Lord, you will protect my vehicle bumper from careless drivers, drunk and reckless drivers. I'm confident you will make sure I am secure.
Your shield is my seatbelt, and nothing bad will happen to me.

There will be no accidents near my car because you will command your angels to protect me. I will not be terrified to drive on the road since my bumper is protected and my tires are securely fastened. I'm confident that the cherubim and archangel are with me.
I pray in the powerful name of Jesus Christ.
Amen.

Weekly Reflection

Private bodyguards and security teams are likely to be costly to hire. As Christians, we don't have to be concerned about such costs because we have private protection from God. The Lord is watching over every part of our life.

God will shield us from all harm and danger. (Psalm 121:8) says, "The LORD will keep your going out and your coming in from this time forth and forevermore." There is nothing that has the power to separate us from our watchful God. As you go through your day, rest assured that God will watch over you. Take a moment to express gratitude to God for overseeing every aspect of your existence.

Do you wish to ask God for a particular favor? Do you require protection from an evil plot or individual? Bring your request for protection to God in prayer.

1ST DAY: BIBLE VERSE OF THE DAY: "He will command his angels concerning you, to guard you. (Luke 4:10).

Reflect on this verse.

2ND DAY: BIBLE VERSE OF THE DAY: "It is the Lord who goes before you. He will be with you; he will not leave you or forsake you. Do not fear or be dismayed." (Deuteronomy 31:8).

Take a moment to express gratitude to God for never abandoning you.

3RD DAY: BIBLE VERSE OF THE DAY: "You are a hiding place for me; you preserve me from trouble; you surround me with shouts of deliverance. I will instruct you and teach you in the way you should go; I will counsel you with my eye upon you." (Psalm 32:7-8).

God is our hiding place and He provides us with a safe haven. When was the last time you found refuge in God or His people?

What role can you play in assisting people in your community to find refuge in God?

4TH DAY: BIBLE VERSE OF THE DAY: "And I will be to her a wall of fire all around, declares the Lord, and I will be the glory in her midst." (Zechariah 2:5).

What do you think it means that God will build a wall of fire around you?

5TH DAY: BIBLE VERSE OF THE DAY: "Guarding the paths of justice and watching over the way of his saints. Then you will understand righteousness and justice and equity, every good path." (Proverbs 2:8-9).

Reflect on God's Word.

6TH DAY: BIBLE VERSE OF THE DAY: "The eyes of the Lord are in every place, keeping watch on the evil and the good." (Proverbs 15:3).

What does this Bible verse teach you about God?

7TH DAY: Time of reflection. "You hem me in, behind and before, and lay your hand upon me." (Psalm 139:5).

Do you feel restricted—hemmed in by whatever's going on around you? If so, what is causing your restriction?

God has hemmed you in. Write or say a prayer thanking God for hemming you in.

BENEDICTION: "The LORD will watch over your coming and going both now and forevermore." Psalm 121:8).

WEEK FORTY-THREE: PRAYER FOR SAFETY AND PROTECTION

Heavenly Father, the Defender,

Shalom, the God of peace, you reign in all aspects of life. I appreciate your kindness, grace, and love toward me. I come to pray for those who are in danger. Violence is at school, on the road, at the supermarket, in the workplace, and in the street. But, Holy Father, You are a God who hates violence. Violence is everywhere. When we read your Words, it clearly declares that violence continually arouses your anger. When you created the world, you never meant it to be so violent. We know it is the sins of our first parents that caused so much hatred in our society. A person who brings violence against his or her brother is covered with shame and will be destroyed forever according to your Word. Even though Peter wanted to defend you from the enemies, you rebuked him and asked him to put the sword back. You said to Peter in (Matthew 26:52), “Put your sword back into its place. For all who take the sword will perish by the sword.”

I come to you to pray for the children in my community, Lord. It is difficult for youngsters to cope in such a hostile environment. I fear the effect of violence on their brains and personalities. However, you have promised to protect your children from all threats so I have no need to be concerned.

Lord, I depend on you day and night because You are my protector, and you never sleep nor slumber. Thank you for answering my prayer. I pray in the mighty name of Jesus.

Amen.

Weekly Reflection

My husband and I traveled to Israel for a 20-day spiritual pilgrimage with a group from the Salvation Army denomination in 1995. I visited numerous places and it was an unforgettable experience. Among all the places I visited, Golgotha was the most remarkable to me. Golgotha is located outside of the old city of Jerusalem and has a skull-shaped appearance. It is the place where the Lord was crucified.

It was quite an experience for me to stand and walk in this place where Jesus had been beaten, humiliated, mocked, and made fun of while clad in a purple gown.
As I wandered around, I reflected on Jesus and tried to envision Jesus carrying His heavy cross to be crucified. What kept coming to mind was that through it all, Jesus did not retaliate. He had the power and He could have called 12 legions of angels to destroy the enemies. He didn't do it. He has nothing to do with violence. Jesus's message was that His kingdom would be spiritual and not political.

Furthermore, He encouraged Christians to show consideration for even their enemies, returning blessings for cursing. "If someone slaps you on one cheek, turn to them the other also. If someone takes your coat, do not withhold your shirt from them." (Luke 6:29 NIV). Paul said, "Do not repay anyone evil for evil. Be careful to do what is right in the eyes of everyone." (Romans 12:17 NIV).

Have you ever been in a situation where you encountered hostility? It could have been on the road, at work, or at home.
What was your response? Was your reaction one of rage, withdrawal, compromise, retaliation, or one where you display your faith in God?
Many people are walking around angry with violence in their minds. Do you know

anyone who is always hostile and quick to anger? It might be a family member, someone in your community, or a person who has done you wrong. What can you do to maybe help this person and increase your love for that person?

1ST DAY: BIBLE VERSE OF THE DAY: "The Lord tests the righteous, but his soul hates the wicked and the one who loves violence." (Psalm 11:5).

Reflect on His Words.

2ND DAY: BIBLE VERSE OF THE DAY: "Then Jesus said to him, 'Put your sword back into its place. All who take the sword will perish by the sword. Do you think that I cannot appeal to my Father, and he will at once send me more than twelve legions of angels? But how then should the Scriptures be fulfilled, that it must be so?'" (Matthew 26:52-54).

What do these Bible verses teach you about God?

3RD DAY: BIBLE VERSE OF THE DAY: "Do not envy a man of violence and do not choose any of his ways." (Proverbs 3:31).

At times, our society appears to be obsessed with violence. There is a lot of violence in the media, and many of us are drawn to it. After a while, we seem to become accustomed to it and it may no longer bother us as much. At times, a situation of significant magnitude might get our attention and we are temporarily affected before moving on. It seems to be a recurring pattern.

In what ways might you be enamored with violence?

4TH DAY: BIBLE VERSE OF THE DAY: "Violence shall no more be heard in your land, devastation or destruction within your borders; you shall call your walls Salvation, and your gates Praise." (Isaiah 60:18).

Reflect on God's Words.

5TH DAY: BIBLE VERSE OF THE DAY: "Why do you pass judgment on your brother? Or you, why do you despise your brother? For we will all stand before the judgment seat of God; for it is written, 'As I live,' says the Lord, 'every knee shall bow to me, and every tongue shall confess to God.' So then each of us will give an account of himself to God. Therefore let us not pass judgment on one another any longer, but rather decide never to put a stumbling block or hindrance in the way of a brother." (Romans 14:10-13).

What do these Bible verses teach you about God and what it means to be a Christian?

6TH DAY: BIBLE VERSE OF THE DAY: "To speak evil of no one, to avoid quarreling, to be gentle, and to show perfect courtesy toward all people." (Titus 3:2).

What do you think it means "to speak evil of no one"?

7TH DAY: Take a moment to say a special prayer for gun violence around the world. There's gun violence in our homes, schools, and many of our communities. Pray also for those who live in constant fear as a result of their experiences with numerous tragedies.

BENEDICTION: "The LORD bless you and keep you; the LORD make his face to shine upon you and be gracious to you; the LORD lift up his countenance upon you and give you peace." (Numbers 6:24-26).

WEEK FORTY-FOUR: SLOW DOWN! AND FOCUS ON JESUS!

Eternal God, I want to always praise you because you are my King and My Savior.

I come to seek your assistance to set my priority to stay at you to adore you, like Mary who has chosen the good portion to be with you, to listen to you, and has a good relationship with you. That is my desire, Lord.

My desire, Yahweh, is to be with you, to walk in obedience, to follow your command, to listen to your Word, and to have an intimate relationship with you.

I command the spirit of distraction, the spirit of lack of concentration, the spirit of worries, and the emotional spirit to get away from me in the name of Jesus. I want to have the right priorities and always keep my focus on you.

I yearn to dwell in Your presence. Help me to prioritize reading my Bible, praying, and seeking your kingdom first, and everything else will fall into place. Unlike Martha, I want to stop running around and handling all of the details. I want to concentrate on You, Lord. I want to have a greater connection with You.

Today, I choose to stay at your feet, where there is satisfaction, restoration, and deliverance. I ask all these in the glorious name of Jesus.

Amen.

Weekly Reflection

Many of us find it difficult to slow down.

Many of us work hard and long hours and find it difficult to take time off or go on vacation. When we finally take a vacation, we frequently bring our work with us, either psychologically or literally. Taking time off for oneself or one's family is quite vital. When you take time off or go on vacation and actually leave your work behind, you tend to feel less stressed and anxious. If you have children, taking time off to spend quality time with them has many benefits for your children, such as building a stronger connection with them. Overall, taking time off to spend with your children, your husband, family, and friends helps to deepen and strengthen your relationship with them.

Are you someone who is constantly on the move? Someone who never gets time to unwind or take a vacation? When was the last time you took some time off for yourself or your family?

What about your time with God? It's the same thing. Spending time with God will allow you to build a better relationship with God.

When was the last time you spent time alone with your God in a peaceful setting?

Many of us struggle to find 15 minutes to spend alone with Him. Do you know the story of Martha and Mary from the Bible? (Luke 10:38-42) discusses two sisters, Martha and Mary, and how they both reacted differently when Jesus came to visit their home. Both of them serve, but Mary recognizes the importance and necessity of choosing to be with Christ at His feet. The Lord has spoken and He said, slow down. He doesn't want you to become distracted, as Martha was.

Be still, because God wants to discuss your current situation with you.

He wants to reveal your future to you. He wants to give you the right direction for your life and your family's life. How can you hear His voice if you are constantly on the move? Have you ever asked yourself, "Have I been standing still?" When was the last time you stood still? Take some time today to be still in God's presence.

Give God more time than you usually do.

Spend some time listening to God and considering what He is saying to you.

1ST DAY: BIBLE VERSE OF THE DAY: "Be still, and know that I am God. I will be exalted among the nations, I will be exalted in the earth!" (Psalm 46:10).

Reflect on God's Words.

2ND DAY: BIBLE VERSE OF THE DAY: "For thus said the Lord God, the Holy One of Israel, 'In returning and rest you shall be saved in quietness and in trust shall be your strength.' But you were unwilling." (Isaiah 30:15).

Take some time to simply have an open discussion and a spirit-filled moment with your Creator.

3RD DAY: BIBLE VERSE OF THE DAY: "The Lord is near to all who call on him, to all who call on him in truth." (Psalm 145:18).

Take a moment now to pray for divine intervention to assist you in keeping your priorities straight and your focus on God.

4TH DAY: BIBLE VERSE OF THE DAY: "I believe that I shall look upon the goodness of the Lord in the land of the living! Wait for the Lord; be strong, and let your heart take courage; wait for the Lord!" (Psalm 27:13-14).

Is God waiting on you or are you waiting on Him at this time in your life? Think about it.

5TH DAY: BIBLE VERSE OF THE DAY: "Teach me, and I will be silent; make me understand how I have done astray." (Job 6:24).

Take a moment to tell God what is most important to you.

6TH DAY: BIBLE VERSE OF THE DAY: "The Lord will fight for you, and you have only to be silent." (Exodus 14:14).

What does this Bible verse reveal to you?

7TH DAY: Take a moment to repeat this prayer: "Most merciful Father, help me not to be distracted. I want to grow deeper and deeper with you. I want to always trust Your plan for my life. My desire is to be close to you and be like you in the precious name of Jesus. Amen."

BENEDICTION: "And the peace of God, which surpasses all understanding, will guard your hearts and your minds in Christ Jesus." (Philippians 4).

WEEK FORTY-FIVE: PRAY FOR HEALING FROM PAIN AND A BROKEN HEART

Dear Heavenly, Mighty Savior,

You are worthy to be praised. The heavens declare your glory and the sky proclaims your handiwork. Everything you have created is great.

Abba Father, I need you more than ever to heal my broken heart. You love me so much that you die for me. I know you won't let the devil destroy my life.

As the All-Knowing One, you are aware of the pain that deception causes me. I feel embarrassed and ashamed. Yahweh, please have mercy on me.

Lord, keep me close and let your limitless love surround me. Today, in the precious name of Jesus, I want to exchange fear for peace, sadness for joy, and weakness for strength. I pray in Jesus' name. Amen.

Weekly Reflection

Have you been deceived, played, manipulated, or given false promises and, as a result, felt humiliated and hurt? Perhaps it was done by one of your friends, coworkers, a family member, boyfriend, or spouse?

You probably felt tricked by someone you trusted and ended up with the wrong group of people or in the wrong place.
There are numerous things or reasons that can cause us to be hurt and heartbroken. Have you moved on from the humiliation and pain, or are you still living in the past?

Perhaps this person and the hurt are always on your mind and you're replaying the situation in your head all the time or even on and off. It can be challenging but necessary to learn to allow your pain and heartache not to take control of your heart and your life as a whole.
(Colossians 3:13) states the following: "Bear with one another and, if one has a complaint against another, forgive each other; as the Lord has forgiven you, so you also must forgive." What are the chances of you overcoming these emotional barriers? Have you prayed to God about this matter?

1ST DAY: BIBLE VERSE OF THE DAY: "He will wipe away every tear from their eyes and death shall be no more, neither shall there be mourning nor crying, nor pain anymore, for the former things have passed away." (Revelation 21:4).

God will wipe your tears away. Have you recently been through heartbreak or emotional pain? What do you need to get off your chest today?

2ND DAY: BIBLE VERSE OF THE DAY: "God is our refuge and strength, a very present help in trouble. Therefore, we will not fear though the earth gives way.

Though the mountains be moved into the heart of the sea." (Psalm 46:1-2).

God is our refuge and strength, a constant aid in times of distress. Think of a time when God did something remarkable for you. Choose to spend time now reflecting on God's faithfulness to you and how He provided you with refuge in your time of need.

3RD DAY: BIBLE VERSE OF THE DAY: "We are afflicted in every way, but not crushed; perplexed, but not driven to despair; persecuted, but not forsaken, struck down, but not destroyed." (2 Corinthians 4:8-9).

What do these Bible verses reveal to you?

4TH DAY: BIBLE VERSE OF THE DAY: "I am weary with my crying out; my throat is parched. My eyes grow dim with waiting for my God." (Psalm 69:3).

Take a moment to reflect on God's Words.

5TH DAY: BIBLE VERSE OF THE DAY: "You who have made me see many troubles and calamities will revive me again; from the depths of the earth you will bring me up again." (Psalm 71:20).

Write or say a prayer to God thanking Him for continuously bringing you the calamities that revitalize you.

6TH DAY: BIBLE VERSE OF THE DAY: "Come to me, all who labor and are heavy laden, and I will give you rest. Take my yoke upon you, and learn from me, for I am gentle and l owly in heart, and you will find rest for your souls." (Matthew 11:28).

What does this Bible verse teach you?

7TH DAY: Repeat this short prayer: "Dear Lord, according to your loving kindness, fill my hurting heart with peace and joy. Your joy is my strength. Amen."

BENEDICTION: "And the peace of God, which surpasses all understanding, will guard your hearts and your minds in Christ Jesus." (Philippians 4:7).

WEEK FORTY-SIX: NO CHAINS OR PRISON BARS CAN STOP ME FROM MY DESTINY!

Dear Sovereign God,

The mighty warrior! You are my God and my Lord. Be magnified for you are worthy to be praised. I bow before you to confess my sins and thank you for victory over every chain. God, there's power in your name. I thank you for allowing me to triumph over all prison bars I have come across.

Joseph was in prison and there he faced terrible difficulties. He was falsely accused and was forgotten. However, in one day, You changed his situation, his story changed, and his life changed. He was promoted to the head of the department. Yes, Lord, you were with Joseph and blessed everything he oversaw.

You even opened Potiphar's eyes and he noticed everything and elevated Joseph to the highest position in his household.

Open doors in my life that were blocked for many years. I wish to overcome any obstacles that impede me from progressing. I wish to be redeemed, in the name of Jesus Christ.

Today, I claim liberation for myself and my family from the bonds that bind us. Lord, I declare freedom from chains of negative attitudes, negative thinking, alcoholism, smoking, drug use, and idleness.

Lord, I beseech you to free them from the bonds of addiction, unexplained bodily ailments, anxiety, and uncertainty. Lord, I know many are stuck in a mental prison. Lord, in the name of Jesus, deliver them.

I know that with you, Lord, anything is possible.

I transport the verdict from the throne of Jesus, the mighty warrior against every spirit of obstruction, impasse, obstacle, spirit of setback to fall unto the ocean in the mighty name of Jesus.

I command any prison of oppression, and turmoil to withdraw from my life in the name of Jesus. I apply the blood of Jesus over my life and my family for safety and protection.

In the name of Jesus, I pray. Amen.

Weekly Reflection

Spiritual prisons and chains are evil things that stop a person from making progress and getting out of their bonds.

Most people who are trapped in a spiritual prison find it difficult to progress in life. Set free that person who is imprisoned by whatever is holding them back from their future in Christ. For instance, not forgiving yourself for past abuse, addiction, grief, and sadness. Other examples can be dwelling on negative issues and rumors, as well as worrying about what others might be saying about you. It can be self-doubt, or even a failed relationship.

If a person feels like they are always being watched, has a fixed mindset and fate, and never blossoms, they are in a spiritual cage or are in chains. These cages and chains can ruin your blessings and convert them to dirt. The Bible says, "The thief comes only to steal and kill and destroy; I have come that they may have life, and have it to the full" (John 10:10 NIV). We are held captive by our sins. Without Christ, we will continue to be prisoners, tied to our sins and ignorance.

What kind of prison are you in today? What are you bound to today? You could be bound by self-doubt, toxic relationships, or addiction. Tell Jesus about your prison, about the chain that surrounds you, and that you need Him to shatter.

By calling on Jesus's name, any chains can be broken. Believe that your spiritual cage can be broken if you believe strongly enough. The Bible says in (Acts 12:7–8), "And behold, an angel of the Lord stood next to him, and a light shone in the cell. He struck Peter on the side and woke him, saying, 'Get up quickly.' And the chains fell off his hands. And the angel said to him, 'Dress yourself and put on your sandals.' And he did so. And he said to him, 'Wrap your cloak around you and follow me.'" In these two verses, we see that the angels did two things: one, they woke Peter up and broke the chain that kept him captive; and second, they gave him instruction. Has God broken the chain that is keeping you captive? Has God broken the chain that has held you captive? Have you received directions from God regarding your next step in life? Spend a few moments praying to God to break every chain in your life.
Ask God to remove you from captivity. Finally, pray for a heart to be obedient to accepting direction and instruction from God.

1ST DAY: BIBLE VERSE OF THE DAY: "But before all this they will lay their hands on you and persecute you, delivering you up to the synagogues and prisons, and you will be brought before kings and governors for my name's sake." (Luke 21:12).
Reflect on God's Word.

2ND: DAY BIBLE VERSE OF THE DAY: "Do not fear what you are about to suffer, Behold, the devil is about to throw some of you into prison, that you may be tested, and for ten days you will have tribulation, Be faithful unto death, and I will give you the crown of life." (Revelation 2:10). We are tested every day with the temptation to do what we know is wrong. When was the last time you felt tested by the devil?

3RD DAY: BIBLE VERSE OF THE DAY: "He brought them out of darkness and the shadow of death, and burst their bonds apart." (Psalm 107:14).

What does this Bible verse teach you about God?

4TH DAY: BIBLE VERSE OF THE DAY: "But during the night an angel of the Lord opened the prison doors and brought them out." (Acts 5:19).

Take a moment now to pray that the plan for your deliverance and advancement will take hold and be effective.

5TH DAY: BIBLE VERSE OF THE DAY: "Be Still and know that I am God." (Psalm 46:10).

Reflect on God's Word.

6TH DAY: BIBLE VERSE OF THE DAY: "I am the LORD, I have called you in righteousness, I have taken you by the hand and kept you; I have given you as a covenant to the people, a light to the nations, to open the eyes that are blind, to bring out the prisoners from the dungeon, from the prison those who sit in darkness." (Isaiah 42:7).

Write or say a prayer to God, asking Him to open your eyes so you can see Jesus.

7TH DAY: Today is the day! Arise, and cry out to God for deliverance from all obstacles and chains in your life, big and small.

BENEDICTION: "And the peace of God, which surpasses all understanding, will guard your hearts and your minds in Christ Jesus." (Philippians 4:7).

WEEK FORTY-SEVEN: THE LORD'S MIGHTY HANDS ARE ON OUR CHILDREN

Precious Lord, we come before you to praise and worship you for your love toward our children. Thank you for giving us these precious gifts. Everyone is very important before you and is equally loved by you. Yes, Lord, you promise a good plan and wonderful purpose for each of their lives.

Abba Father, You know the world is broken, and places that we want to believe are safe are not always safe, Lord.

I pray that our children will not be afraid because you are with them. Help them to feel your presence, and give them the strength they need. Give us serenity as we entrust our children in your capable hands, knowing that you are always by their side. We worry as parents, and fear wants to grasp us, therefore, we ask for peaceful hearts, Lord. Lord, I asked that you be with them especially when they are at school. You can intervene and change the situation to make the school the safest place for our children.

Yahweh, please keep our children safe from physical violence and abuse in all forms. God, please keep their minds from being corrupted by Satan's lies. Help them speak up for what is right and protect their minds from things that might corrupt them. Please, God, give them the strength to resist the urge to accept the world and its values that are not Yours.

Lord, bless the teachers and grant them patience and wisdom so they can educate our children. If they do not believe in you, I hope that You will open their hearts to believe in Your power, so that they will only show and direct our children in ways that are right in your eyes.

I prayed that you would assist us in being good role models for our children. Please, help us to live a life that is right by You.

In the name of Jesus Christ, the King of kings and Lord of lords, I pray.

Amen.

Weekly Reflection

Each of us has had role models or mentors throughout our lives.
We were not always aware of our role models and the impact they had on our lives and characters, whether that impact was favorable or negative. Although there is only one perfect role model, Jesus Christ. God wants us to set an example for His children through the way we live our lives as Christians.

A child's likelihood of mimicking an adult's good deeds increases when that adult serves as a positive role model.
In every aspect of your life, from the way you treat your body, to the relationship you have with Jesus Christ, you have the opportunity to set an example for a child and influence their growth. The Bible says in (Proverbs 22:6), "Train up a child in the way he should go; even when he is old he will not depart from it."

How do you serve as a role model for your children and the children in your family, church, and community? What do your daily acts teach God's children, including your own children?

Sometimes, we experience challenges and tribulations that leave us dealing with shame, illness, and pain.
As a result, we may believe that God has abandoned and left us.
This appears to be the case for some of us, particularly when we are facing excruciating bodily pains and traumas that seem to have no end in sight.
Have you recently felt this way?
During those times, it is especially hard to be a good example of Christ.
What kind of role models do you provide for God's children, including your own

children, during times of adversity? (1 Peter 2:21) states, "For to this you have been called, because Christ also suffered for you, leaving you an example, so that you might follow in his steps." Surviving and continuing to witness for Christ in the face of challenges and tragedies demands fortitude, a positive attitude, and, most importantly faith and connection with God.

Do you believe that you have courage, a positive attitude, faith, and a connection to the Lord our Savior?

1ST DAY: BIBLE VERSE OF THE DAY: "Remember your leaders, those who spoke to you the word of God. Consider the outcome of their way of life, and imitate their faith." (Hebrews 13:7). Reflect on your spiritual journey. Have you had a Christian mentor, a spiritual father, or a mother? It may have been your pastor, a friend, or a member of your family. What is the name of that individual, and what is the most essential lesson you learned from them?

2ND DAY: BIBLE VERSE OF THE DAY: "Then Jesus said to the crowds and to his disciples, 'The scribes and the Pharisees sit on Moses's seat, so do and observe whatever they tell you, but not the works they do. For they preach, but do not practice.'' (Matthew 23:1-3).

What do these Bible verses teach you?

3RD DAY: BIBLE VERSE OF THE DAY: "The strong right arm of the Lord is raised in triumph. The strong right arm of the Lord has done glorious things!" (Psalm 118:16). God performs miracles with His mighty hand so that the people of the world would know that the Lord's hand is powerful. What have you been worried about recently in terms of your children, grandchildren, or the children around you?

What issues do you wish to present to God on behalf of your children?

4TH DAY: BIBLE VERSE OF THE DAY: "All your children shall be taught by the Lord, and great shall be the peace of your children." (Isaiah 54:13).

Now is the time to declare and decree your victory over your children.

5TH DAY: BIBLE VERSE OF THE DAY: "Jesus called the children to him and said, 'Let the little children come to me and do not hinder them, for to such belongs the kingdom of heaven.' And he laid his hands on them and went away." (Matthew 19:14-15)

Have you brought your children to Jesus Christ?

What do you do to prepare your children to confront life's challenges?

Do you pray with your children on a regular basis to reassure them that God's strong hand is on them?

6TH DAY: BIBLE VERSE OF THE DAY: "Behold, I have engraved you on the palms of my hands; your walls are continually before me." (Isaiah 49:16).

Take a moment to reflect on God's Words.

7TH DAY: Take a moment to glorify God for his tender grace and mercy toward your children this year.

BENEDICTION: "Surely goodness and mercy shall follow me all the days of my life, and I shall dwell in the house of the Lord forever." (Psalm 23:6)

WEEK FORTY-EIGHT: I LONG TO BE HOLY O LORD!

Heavenly Father,

I hail you Jesus and worship you, the King of kings. Yes, you are a holy God.

As your child, I long to be holy too. Please, cleanse my heart and my filthy thoughts.

I am a sinner and come short of your glory.

Abba Father, I cry as King David cried: "Create in me a pure heart, O God, and renew a steadfast spirit within me." (Psalm 51:10 NIV).

I ask that you uproot and burn with holy fire all the things that are unpleasant so that I may be set free today.

I bow at your feet, waiting for the holy fire so that I might be led by the Holy Spirit, bear the fruit of the spirit, and live a godly life. Your Words in (Luke 22:56) refer to the servant girl recognizing Peter as being with you.

I want the entire world to know that I am with You.

I want to establish a close relationship with you so that wherever I go the world can know that I live a holy life and that I belong to you. What I long for and desire is holiness. I want to experience holiness everywhere I go since that is the key to having a joyful life. Knowing you and living a holy life is everything I long for, and I pray in Jesus's wonderful name.

Amen.

Weekly Reflection

According to the Bible, God is a holy God. We cannot compare ourselves to God because we do not have divine attributes such as omnipotence, omniscience, and omnipresence, among others. God is holy and perfect, and He is utterly unlike the imperfect world in which we live. God is righteous at all times. We have a fundamental obligation as Christians to conduct ourselves in a holy manner. Since it is said, "But as he who called you is holy, you also be holy in all your conduct, since it is written, 'You shall be holy, for I am holy'" (1 Peter 1:15-16). God's call to holiness is echoed in this verse from the Bible.

Despite our imperfections, we are nevertheless capable of leading a holy life. What does it mean to be holy and live a holy life? Some of us hold the mistaken belief that we must achieve perfection in order to lead a holy life. No, that's not the case at all.

Only God is perfect. To live a holy life means committing oneself to God and to the service of others. A holy life necessitates self-control, concentration on God and His teachings, and moral awareness.

Those who identify as Christian should prioritize living a holy life. Are you living a life that is holy? If not, what can you do to be holy?

1ST DAY: BIBLE VERSE OF THE DAY: "Since we have these promises, beloved, let us cleanse ourselves from every defilement of body and spirit, bringing holiness to completion in the fear of God." (2 Corinthians 7:1).

Take some time to reflect on God's Word.

2ND DAY: BIBLE VERSE OF THE DAY: "Speak to the entire assembly of Israel and say to them: 'Be holy because I, the Lord your God, am holy.'" (Leviticus 19:2 NIV).

3RD DAY: BIBLE VERSE OF THE DAY: "Strive for peace with everyone, and for the holiness without which no one will see the Lord." (Hebrews 12:14).

What do you think are the benefits of being holy?

4TH DAY: BIBLE VERSE OF THE DAY: "How can a young man keep his way pure? By guarding it according to your word." Psalm 119:9).

What can you do as a Christian today to maintain a holy life?

5TH DAY: BIBLE VERSE OF THE DAY: "Who saved us and called us to a holy calling, not because of our works but because of his own purpose and grace, which he gave us in Christ Jesus before the ages began." (2 Timothy 1:9).

Take a moment to reflect on God's Word.

6TH DAY: BIBLE VERSE OF THE DAY: "Search me, O God, and know my heart! Try me and know my thoughts! And see if there be any grievous way in me, and lead me in the way everlasting!" (Psalm 139:23-24).

Using these Bible verses, write or say a prayer to God. If you prefer, you can simply pray the words of these Bible texts.

7TH DAY. Holiness is not achieved overnight, and it is not a one-time event, but a continuous practice and commitment. Do not become disheartened. Instead, spend time with God and pray for holiness.

BENEDICTION: "I appeal to you therefore, brothers, by the mercies of God, to present your bodies as a living sacrifice, holy and acceptable to God, which is your spiritual worship." (Romans 12:1).

WEEK FORTY-NINE: WATCH OVER ME LORD—BEDTIME PRAYER

Mighty God, I approach before your throne to cry out hosannas in the mighty name of Jesus. You are in control of the universe. Blessed be your holy name.

Your Word teaches me that I shall sleep peacefully because, even though I am alone, O Lord, you will keep me secure.

You promise that you will keep me in perfect peace. Yahweh, I know that You are a promise keeper. So, do not let unpleasant dreams haunt me. I pray that you remove the nightmares that keep me and my loved ones at night. You are my keeper. I trust you with my sleep and my dreams. Take complete control of my conscious mind, Mighty Warrior. As the excellent shepherd who never sleeps nor slumbers, I pray for Your whole presence.

Sometimes, I find myself awakened in the middle of the night and can't sleep again. Please, rebuke all the bad thoughts and feelings that prevent me from sleeping. Right now, I seek your peace and a quiet mind. Please, prevent Satan from coming and interfering with my sleep in the name of Jesus.

Precious God, I know you are my only source of strength and protection.
Please, sanctify everywhere and every place I put my head to rest or sleep with your blood that was shared on the Calvary Cross.

In the name of Jesus Christ, the powerful Savior, all wicked and satanic weapons sent at me in my dreams or preventing me from sleeping are rendered ineffective and returned to the sender. I request that You keep my home safe from intruders.

In Jesus's name.

Amen.

Weekly Reflection

What is your definition of the word "nightmare"? What images spring to mind when you hear the word "nightmare"? A nightmare, in my opinion, is a frightening, unpleasant dream. Some people experience various symptoms as a result of having a nightmare. For example, some people experience panic or anxiety after having a nightmare and having trouble sleeping as a result. Some people's hearts beat faster than usual, while others have no symptoms at all and can quickly return to sleep.

I have read about several strategies that one can do to return to sleep after having a nightmare. Personally, I employ the strategy of devoting time to prayer and, on occasion, reading (Psalm 3). What do you normally do after having a nightmare?

Do you think a nightmare is a form of communication with God? Well, let us start with: What are the ways that God communicates with us? Specifically, what are some ways that God communicates with you? God communicates with us through the Bible, so when we take the time to read the Bible, we are communicating with God. God communicates with us through prayer, a song, and a trusted follower of Christ expressing God's Words, our own experiences, or the experiences of others.

The Bible says that God communicates with some of us also through dreams and visions. The Bible contains numerous references to dreams. One example is (1 Samuel 28:15): "Then Samuel said to Saul, 'Why have you disturbed me by bringing me up?' Saul answered, 'I am in great distress, for the Philistines are warring against me, and God has turned away from me and answers me no more, either by prophets or by dreams. Therefore I have summoned you to tell me what I shall do.'"

Abimelech, and Nebuchadnezzar through dreams or visions, according to the Bible. Have you ever had a dream or vision in which God spoke to you? If so, what was the message you received from God? What are the most frequent ways you receive God's message?

What is your favorite way to communicate with God?

1ST DAY: BIBLE VERSE OF THE DAY: "In peace I will both lie down and sleep, for you alone, O Lord, make me dwell in safety." (Psalm 4:8).

Are you a person who experiences nightmares on a regular basis or often feels distressed at night? Perhaps you know someone who is in constant turmoil at night. If you ever feel distressed at night, remember that prayer is our most powerful weapon against all types of distress. Write or utter a prayer to God for yourself or someone else, asking Him to keep you safe at night and to help you sleep peacefully.

2ND DAY: BIBLE VERSE OF THE DAY: "So if the Son sets you free, you will be free indeed." (John 8:36).

Reflect on God's Words. What does it mean to be truly free as a Christ follower?

3RD DAY: BIBLE VERSE OF THE DAY: "Blessed be the Lord, my rock, who trains my hands for war, and my fingers for battle." (Psalm 144:1).

Write or say a prayer of appreciation to God for all He has done for you this year.

4TH DAY: BIBLE VERSE OF THE DAY: "For God does speak—now one way, now another though no one perceives it. In a dream, in a vision of the night, when deep sleep falls on people as they slumber in their beds, he may speak in their ears and terrify them with warnings, to turn them from wrongdoing and keep them from pride, to preserve them from the pit, their lives from perishing by the sword." (Job 33:14-18 NIV).

Take a moment to reflect on God's Words.

5TH DAY: BIBLE VERSE OF THE DAY: "In hope of eternal life, which God, who never lies, promised before the ages began." (Titus 1:2).

Is the prospect of heaven something that you're looking forward to? Do you have hope in eternal life? Is there anything you can do right now to ensure your place in heaven tomorrow?

6TH DAY: BIBLE VERSE OF THE DAY: "And there will be signs in sun and moon and stars, and on the earth distress of nations in perplexity because of the roaring of the sea and the waves." (Luke 21:25).

Reflect on God's Words.

7TH DAY: Today, take a moment to reflect on your favorite Bible verse.

BENEDICTION: "And the peace of God, which surpasses all understanding, will guard your hearts and your minds in Christ Jesus." (Philippians 4:7).

WEEK FIFTY: A PRAYER FOR SINGLES

Most High God,

I bow before you to confess my sins and to worship you for your love and your kindness. Everything I have needed, you have always provided. You are a great God and everything about you is great and deserves to be praised. Thank you for changing my story from singleness to married woman. I wanted my own companion. You say, ask and it shall be given. So, I asked you to pick my soulmate, the one that you wanted me to marry. I took you at your Word because Your Word will never fail. Lord, I thank you for providing me with my husband, a man of God.

You knew that Adam would be lonely, and that is why you made a companion for him.God, I come to you bringing a dear sister in Christ to you in prayer. I know that it is not your desire for her to be alone forever. This is your promise to your people. I know that you have a great plan to bring her a companion. You will choose the right person that you want for her. Father, you took time out to find a wife for your servant Isaac, so I know that you can do it for her as well. Singleness can be exhausting and lonely, especially when it is unwelcome. You sent Boaz for Ruth, and I pray that you will send a person for my dear sister. I pray in the mighty name of Jesus.

Amen.

Weekly Reflection

Various women have different opinions about marriage. Some women believe that marriage is a complex institution. Others remark that it is too much effort, or that it appears to be too much work, and that they are unwilling to commit. Some women love and aspire to their wedding and the honeymoon phases of marriage. They are not really interested in what comes after the honeymoon. Other women want to live free and experience life on their own terms, and they are unwilling to compromise or give up their freedom in order to marry. Then there are those who believe they enjoy the concept of being an independent woman and do not seek male assistance. As a result, marriage is unimportant. They would rather devote their attention to their careers, and being single allows them to do so.

Indeed, some women truly want to remain single and independent forever or for a short time, but others pretend to want to be independent of their friends, coworkers, and family due to societal or cultural pressure to find a husband, in reality, they're lonely and don't believe they can find the good man.

As a result, they decide to play a role and claim to be an "independent woman," when in fact they are not. The importance of marriage has been called into question on numerous occasions. But God's Word says: "Then the LORD God said, 'It is not good that the man should be alone; I will make him a helper fit for him." (Genesis 2:18). What are your thoughts on marriage? Are you wanting to get married if you are single? What do you want in a marriage if you're looking to get married? Are your expectations about marriage realistic?

What words would you use to describe your ideal marriage?

God knew that Adam would be lonely, and provided a companion for him.

Then the LORD God said, "It is not good that the man should be alone; I will make him a helper fit for him."

If you are intended to be married, He has surely created your soulmate and will bring him to you at the appropriate time. What you must do is live a godly life, believe in God and His Words, obey His instructions, and wait for Him.

When God brings you face to face with your husband, you will be able to say "Yes, that is him and repeat the following words." (Genesis 2:23 NIV) says, "This is now bone of my bones and flesh of my flesh." Remember that only God can provide you with a suitable match, and you must be prepared.

If you are single and want to marry, are you psychologically and spiritually prepared? Are you carrying emotional baggage that you need to bring to God in prayer before you consider marriage?

How well are you prepared for marriage?

God has a beautiful plan in store for you. What can you do as a Christian woman to prepare for and await the husband God has planned for you?

Write or say a prayer to God, asking Him to prepare you for marriage so that you will be ready when you meet your future husband.

If you are not single, you can spend some time praying for a sister, daughter, granddaughter, cousin, friend, or member of your church who wishes to marry.

1ST DAY: BIBLE VERSE OF THE DAY: "The Lord your God is in your midst, a mighty one who will save; he will rejoice over you with gladness; he will quiet by his love; he will exult over you with loud singing." (Zephaniah 3:17).

Take a moment to reflect on God's Word.

2ND DAY: BIBLE VERSE OF THE DAY: "Trust in the Lord with all your heart, and do not lean on your own understanding. In all your ways acknowledge him, and he will make straight your paths." (Proverbs 3:5-6).

When looking for something significant, the greatest place to start is prayer.

Close your eyes for five minutes and pray or meditate.

3RD DAY: BIBLE VERSE OF THE DAY: "For the LORD God is a sun and shield; the LORD bestows favor and honor. No good thing does he withhold from those who walk uprightly." (Psalm 84:11).

Allow God's Word to speak to you today:

4TH DAY: BIBLE VERSE OF THE DAY: "What then shall we say to these things? If God is for us, who can be against us?" (Romans 8:31).

Take a few moments to compose or recite a prayer thanking Him for being there for us.

5TH DAY: BIBLE VERSE OF THE DAY: "Call to me and I will answer you, and will tell you great and hidden things that you have not known." (Jeremiah 33:3).

What does this Bible verse teach you?

6TH DAY: BIBLE VERSE OF THE DAY: "But seek ye first the kingdom of God, and his righteousness; and all these things shall be added unto you." (Matthew 6:33).

What does God want you to do after reading this passage?

7TH DAY: Spend some time praising and worshiping God. Then close your eyes and open your heart to receive the blessings that He has stored for you.

BENEDICTION: "And the peace of God, which surpasses all understanding, will guard your hearts and your minds in Christ Jesus." (Philippians 4:7).

WEEK FIFTY-ONE: A PRAYER FOR LIFE CHANGES AND TRANSFORMATION

Mighty God,

Lord, here I am as your child seeking your presence. You are my father, my friend, my mentor, and my mediator. I am here on behalf of a loved one. You know him by name and nature. I'm praying that he will accept you into his life. It is difficult because he is extremely stubborn, but this type of change can only be found in you.

You are the changer of life, any bad situation can be transformed and become good. There is no person's life that cannot change by You. If you have changed Apostle Paul's life, and transformed the life of Zacchaeus, you can do it for my loved one as well. You can perform a miracle for him. He needs to know you and accept you as His personal Savior.

Your Word in (Romans 10:9) says that "because, if you confess
with your mouth that Jesus is Lord and believe in your heart that God raised him from the dead, you will be saved."

Please, touch his heart and help him to confess you as the only Savior. Change his negative mind, attitude, and behavior to something positive.
I believe you will change him, renew his mind and stubborn heart for the better.
Father, it breaks my heart to see loved ones perish in sin and degradation.
It's difficult to see a family member becoming spiritually blind, falling into the devil's trap, and seeming unable to escape. Help me, Lord, to be a good example for him. Please, assist me in being a good witness for him.

Thank you in advance for bringing him from chaos to order, from hopelessness to hopefulness. I pray in the beautiful name of Jesus.

Amen.

Weekly Reflection

Are you looking to make a change in your life? Are you dealing with circumstances that have put you in dire need and as a result want to make a change? Perhaps you've realized that you need to make a shift or complete transformation in your life because you don't like the direction you are heading. Maybe you want to make a change in your life in order to achieve a specific goal.

How does one go about bringing about change or transformation in one's life? There is a lot of literature on the issue, and people have approached it in many ways. You may have read about and tried a variety of approaches for making life changes. Some people, for example, read or listen to inspirational stories about making changes, or biographical stories or movies about someone who has made changes. Others have applied strategies or sought professional help to reprogram their life, or even a step-by-step guide to assist them in making required adjustments in their lives. These techniques might be helpful, but transformation occurs from within and it entails more than just changing your words and behavior; it involves your thoughts, attitudes, and emotions.

If you want to change the course of your life, Christ and His Word must be the most essential tools in your life. You can follow different approaches, but Christ is required for true transformation.

The Bible has numerous stories about how God changed people's lives. For example, Zacchaeus, a small man, was the chief tax collector. He is best known for climbing a sycamore tree to see Jesus. As a tax collector, his countrymen detested him. He was reviled. He was saved and given a new life by Jesus. He turned from being a severe tax collector who imposed high taxes on his people to becoming incredibly charitable, giving half of what he owned. Another well-known example is Saul's transformation into Paul. Saul was a persecutor of Christians before becoming Paul. Paul was saved by Jesus Christ and devoted his life to preaching and teaching about the Savior and the gospel.

Which transformation do you want God to bring about in your life today?

To experience true transformation, you must have Christ in your life. What kind of relationship do you have with Jesus Christ? Perhaps there is someone in your home, a family member like your child or spouse. Maybe it is a friend or colleague, someone who needs a true transformation and has not accepted a relationship with Jesus Christ. Take a moment to write or say a prayer to God about this person's situation.

1ST DAY: BIBLE VERSE OF THE DAY: "But to all who did receive him, who believed in his name, he gave the right to become children of God." (John 1:12).

You are a child of God. You are magnificently made, greatly loved, and valuable in His eyes. Today, take a moment to praise God for the privilege of calling Him Father.

2ND DAY: BIBLE VERSE OF THE DAY: "If you confess with your mouth that Jesus is Lord and believe in your heart that God raised him from the dead, you will be saved. For with the heart one believes and is justified, and with the mouth one confesses and is saved." (Romans 10:9-10).

Be still and pause to give thanks to God for His grace and salvation.

3RD DAY: BIBLE VERSE OF THE DAY: "For God so loved the world, that he gave his only Son, that whoever believes in him should not perish but have eternal life." (John 3:16).

Take a minute today to consider God's goodness and faithfulness.

4TH DAY: BIBLE VERSE OF THE DAY: "For all have sinned and fall short of the glory of God." (Romans 3:23).

Reflect on God's blessings and favor today.

5TH DAY: BIBLE VERSE OF THE DAY: "For by grace you have been saved through faith. And this is not your own doing; it is the gift of God." (Ephesians 2:8).

Take a minute to reflect on the last few weeks, and consider how God's grace has helped you recently.

6TH DAY: BIBLE VERSE OF THE DAY: "Because, if you confess with your mouth that Jesus is Lord and believe in your heart that God raised him from the dead, you will be saved." (Romans 10:9).

Have you confessed with your mouth that Jesus is Lord? Do you have faith that God raised Jesus from the dead? Do you believe that you've been saved? What is God leading you to do as a result of reading this Bible verse?

7TH DAY: Bible Verse of the Day: "But understand this, that in the last days there will come times of difficulty. For people will be lovers of self, lovers of money, proud, arrogant, abusive, disobedient to their parents, ungrateful, unholy, heartless."

(2 Timothy 3:1-2).

What does God want you to take away from reading these verses?

BENEDICTION: "Do not conform to the pattern of this world, but be transformed by the renewing of your mind. Then you will be able to test and approve what God's will is his good, pleasing and perfect will." (Romans 12:2).

WEEK FIFTY-TWO: GOD IS THE MAKER AND GIVER OF NEW THINGS FOR THE NEW YEAR

Dear Heavenly Father,

On the last day of this year, I approach your throne to thank you for the marvelous things that you have done. Father, "If You had not been my help; my soul would soon have lived in the land of silence" (Psalm 94:17).

Yahweh, I thank you for your grace and your love that brought me through. O Lord, thank you a million times for your protection, your care, and your guidance.
As I am entering this New Year, I am focusing on the many challenges, uncertainties, worries, and unexpected life changes.
As the God of hope, fill my mind and heart with peace, hope, and joy, so that I can continue to look on you as the Creator of everything.

Fill me with confidence and help me to continue to walk by faith, to excel, to move forward, to shine, and be victorious. Thank you for your favor for this New Year which has no beginning and no end. I ask for all these mercies in the most precious name of Jesus.
Amen.

Weekly Reflection

What is your favorite sport? When was the last time you participated in a sporting event? Was it competitive? Did you take the competition seriously enough? Do you enjoy competing? You may be dreading the start of the New Year due to the baggage you're lugging around with you. This can range from the weight of your past, including fear, diversions, resentment, anger, jealousy, and the burdens of your present. Many of these weights may feel overwhelming to you. Some people see the end of the New Year as an opportunity to start a new race. And everyone in the race wants to win. Therefore, it stands to reason that doing so will motivate them to run with optimism, positivity, and perseverance. Many create goals and resolutions as a result. In order to succeed, remember that you must consciously let go of all unnecessary baggage. It does not happen by itself. You must make an effort to bring the matter to God.

(Hebrews 12:1) states, "Therefore, since we are surrounded by so great a cloud of witnesses, let us also lay aside every weight, and sin which clings so closely, and let us run with endurance the race that is set before us."

Do you have a lot of excess baggage that you need to get rid of? Is it dragging you down and draining your energy?

For this year, what is your plan for releasing some of your burdens? Are you planning to continue carrying your baggage with you? Do you intend to lay aside the unnecessary weight in the New Year, such as a flawed mentality, divisiveness, or jealousy that blocks blessings from coming your way?

Do you want to win your spiritual race or are you just going through the motions? Write down anything that you believe will prevent you from winning this race. For example, you may find it difficult to concentrate on the task at hand. Spend some time writing or reciting a prayer in which you confess and implore God's Holy Spirit to enable and equip you to win this race.

1ST DAY: BIBLE VERSE OF THE DAY: "Therefore, since we are surrounded by so great a cloud of witnesses, let us also lay aside every weight, and sin which clings so closely, and let us run with endurance the race that is set before us, looking to Jesus, the founder and perfecter of our faith, who for the joy that was set before him endured the cross, despising the shame, and is seated at the right hand of the throne of God." (Hebrew 12:1-2).

What do God's Words reveal to you?

2ND DAY: BIBLE VERSE OF THE DAY: "Let us hold fast the confession of our hope without wavering, but he who promised is faithful." (Hebrew 10:23).

Take a moment to reflect on God's Words.

3RD DAY: BIBLE VERSE OF THE DAY: "Peace I leave with you; my peace I give to you. Not as the world gives do I give to you. Let not your hearts be troubled, neither let them be afraid." (John 14:27).

Write or say a prayer thanking God for peace. Take a moment to thank Him for the previous year.

4TH DAY: BIBLE VERSE OF THE DAY: "Do not be anxious about anything, but in everything by prayer and supplication with thanksgiving let your requests be made known to God." (Philippians 4:6).

Do you have anything on your mind as the New Year comes to a close that could be causing you stress?

Do you have any hangovers from the previous year that you'd rather not bring into the New Year?

5TH DAY: BIBLE VERSE OF THE DAY: "Therefore I tell you, whatever you ask in prayer, believe that you have received it, and it will be yours." (Mark 11:24).

Ponder on God's Words. What do you want to ask God today? What do you think you'll need to win the race? You could ask Him to help you rejuvenate your thoughts or to grant you discernment in all aspects of your life. Take a moment to put your request forward.

6TH DAY: BIBLE VERSE OF THE DAY: "The Lord is my shepherd; I shall not want." (Psalm 23:1).

As the first line of your prayer today, repeat this Bible verse.

7TH DAY: Gracious Father, I appreciate everything you've done for me. Assist me in running just on the road you have created for me. Give me the strength to let go of everything that is not of You. Direct my steps to be faith-filled and to always look to you. God, assist me to live a purposeful life and to always be grateful for salvation and Your grace. Amen.

BENEDICTION: "And the peace of God, which surpasses all understanding, will guard your hearts and your minds in Christ Jesus." (Philippians 4:7).

WOMEN'S EMPOWERMENT: DECLARE, SPEAK, AND CLAIM IT

1. I declare that I was created in God's image. As a result, I am lovely, intellectual, gorgeous, and beautiful. (See Genesis 1:27).

2. I declare that I am wonderfully and magnificently made. I am unique. I'm here for a reason. Nobody can look down on me. Amen. (See Psalms 139:14).

3. I declare that I am a child of the King of kings. Therefore, I am a royal princess in the powerful name of Jesus. Amen.

4. I declare that I have received an inheritance, which I predestined in accordance with the will of God. (See 1 Corinthians 1:11).

5. I declare that I will always be at the top, never at the bottom. In the name of Jesus, I am a natural leader. Amen. (See Deuteronomy 28:13).

6. I declare that God has a solid plan for me. In the powerful name of Jesus my Lord, I will flourish and prosper in everything I undertake. (See Jeremiah 29:11).

7. I declare that I am a tree planted by the riverside. I am never dry, and I always produce fruits that last. (See Psalm 1:3).

8. My children, grandchildren, and future generations will continue to shine in the mighty name of Jesus, my Savior. I declare that nothing is too difficult for my God. (See Jeremiah 32:17).

9. I declare that my God is capable of doing immeasurably more than all that I ask or expect, according to His power at work within me. Hallelujah! (See Ephesians 3:20).

10. I declare that I am a chosen race, a royal priesthood, a holy nation, a people for God's own possession, and that God proclaims the excellencies of Him who called me out of darkness into His glorious light. Amen. (See 1 Peter 2:9).

11. I declare that I am God's servant and that His Spirit resides within me. Amen. (See Colossians 3:16).

12. I declare that I am more than a conqueror, in the Lord's name, Amen. (See Romans 8:37).

13. I declare that I am victorious in Jesus Christ, Amen. (See 1 Corinthians 15:57).

14. I declare that the Lord answered my plea, saw my tears, and healed me in the name of Jesus Christ, the Mighty Warrior. Amen. (See 2 Kings 20:5).

15. I declare, my God heals all my diseases. And I am cured in Jesus's strong name, Amen. (See Psalms 103:1-2).

16. I declare that God will multiply my descendants like the stars of heaven and will give all these territories to my descendants. Amen. (See Genesis. 22:17-18).

17. I declare that I shall enjoy my good health and that everything will go well with me, in the wonderful name of Jesus, Amen. (See 3 John 1:2).

18. I declare that no weapon devised against me shall prosper in the great name of Jesus Christ, Amen. (See Isaiah. 54:17).

19. I declare that every voice that rises in judgment against me will be condemned. It is my inheritance and God's vindication. Hallelujah! (See Isaiah. 54:17).

20. I declare that my body is the living God's temple. As a result, I am not alone; I am His. Amen. (See Corinthians 6:19-20).

21. I declare with my lips that Jesus is Lord, and I believe with all my heart that God raised Him from the dead, so that I may be saved. (See Roman 10:9-13).

22. I declare that my God is coming with the clouds, and I will see Him, even those who pierced Him, and all tribes of the earth will wail on account of Him. Amen. (See Revelation 1:7).

ABOUT THE AUTHOR

Edmane Castor was born in a small town called Duveger, near Fonds-des-Nègres in Haiti. She dedicated her life to God at the age of 12. At the age of 23, God spoke to her and called her to become a minister of the gospel in the Salvation Army.

She left her country, her family, and her friends and moved to Jamaica, and joined the Salvation Army Training College.

At the end of her training, she married her spouse and they were both commissioned and ordained as Salvation Army officers (ministers). God dispatched her and her husband to serve in over 22 nations in the Caribbean, Africa, and North America to minister to others.

During her career, she has had the honor and privilege of mentoring, preaching, counseling, advising, and providing social services to thousands of people. She has also helped many individuals work through their problems and grow spiritually and become closer to Christ. She is thankful to God for choosing her , breaking her, molding her, and using her for His purpose and mission.

She is currently a retired minister and a Commissioner of the Salvation Army but is always actively writing about her relationship with God.

Please visit www.edmaneprayerwarrior.com for more information about the author.

Made in United States
North Haven, CT
17 July 2023

39174762R00161